The Twelve Plays of Christmas

The Twelve Plays of Christmas
Original Christian Dramas

Sheryl J. Anderson

Judson Press
Valley Forge

The Twelve Plays of Christmas: Original Christian Dramas
© 1999 by Judson Press, Valley Forge, PA 19482-0851

Library of Congress Cataloguing-in-Publication Data

Anderson, Sheryl J., 1958–
  The twelve plays of Christmas: original Christian dramas/Sheryl J. Anderson
      p.   cm.
ISBN 0-8170-1312-1 (pbk.: alk. paper)
1. Christmas plays, American.   2. Christian drama, American.   I. Title.
PS3551.N3947T88 1999
812'.54—dc21   98-53386

Printed in the U.S.A.

06 05 04 03

10 9 8 7 6 5 4 3 2

To Mark & Sara
and to Mom, Dad, & Eric,
my greatest blessings

Contents

Preface

This book features twelve chancel dramas for Christmas, with a "bonus" drama for Epiphany. For the most part, all the parts in all the plays can be portrayed by an actor of either sex and of any age who is up to the dialogue. Settings are suggested but can certainly be adapted to your playing area, budget, and time constraints. While there are a number of ways of looking at Christmas presented here, the unifying theme is the power of the simplicity of the season. I encourage you to value the power of simplicity in your productions as well, so that the stresses of mounting an elaborate production do not interfere with your communication of the message or with your own enjoyment of the miracle of Christmas.

Love and joy come to you and yours.

Christmas

"Jingle Bells" Revisited

(From Sheryl J. Anderson, *The Twelve Plays of Christmas: Original Christian Dramas*, ©1999 by Judson Press. Reproduced by permission of Judson Press.)

This short, simple presentation is ideal for very young children or a mixed-age group of children.

(The children process in to an instrumental version of "O, Come All Ye Faithful" and line up in the front of the sanctuary.)

READER #1:   The people who walk in darkness will see a great light; those who live in a dark land, the light will shine on them. . . . For a child will be born to us, a son will be given to us; and the government will rest on his shoulders; and his name will be called Wonderful Counselor, Mighty God, Eternal Father, Prince of Peace.

READER #2:   And the angel appeared to the shepherds and said to them, "Do not be afraid; for behold, I bring you good news of a great joy which shall be for all the people; for today in the city of David there has been born for you a Savior, who is Christ the Lord. And this will be a sign for you: you will find a baby wrapped in cloths, and lying in a manger."

CHILDREN: *(Singing)*
Away in a manger, no crib for a bed
The little Lord Jesus lay down his sweet head
The stars in the sky looked down where he lay
The little Lord Jesus asleep on the hay

Be near me, Lord Jesus, I ask you to stay
Close by me forever, and love me, I pray
Bless all the dear children in thy tender care
And take us to heaven to live with thee there

READER #3:   That classic Christmas carol was written by Martin Luther in the sixteenth century. Now, we would like to share a more modern Christmas song with you.

(The accompanist plays the first few bars of the chorus of "Jingle Bells.")

READER #4:   Hey, wait a minute! That's "Jingle Bells."

READER #3:   That's right.

READER #4:   But we can't sing "Jingle Bells" in church.

READER #3: Sure we can. Because when you remember that Jesus is the true reason we celebrate Christmas, everything takes on new meaning. Even a song like "Jingle Bells."

READER #4: But how can we keep Jesus the focus of our celebration if people get distracted by Santa and snow and silly stuff?

READER #3: If you keep Jesus in your heart, you'll keep Jesus in the celebration. And I think I know a way to help you remember that he is part of every Christmas that is celebrated with joy and love. Listen to this.

CHILDREN: *(Singing to the tune of "Jingle Bells")*
Jesus Christ, Jesus Christ
Born this very day
Sent by God to save the world
And wash our sins away
Jesus Christ, Jesus Christ
Our savior and our friend
He's the reason that we're here
Merry Christmas and Amen!

Born in a manger bare
Beneath a shining star
Adored by shepherds poor
And wise men from afar
This little tiny babe,
He was the King of kings
And that's why every Christmas now
We gather and we sing:

Jesus Christ, Jesus Christ
Born this very day
Sent by God to save the world
And wash our sins away
Jesus Christ, Jesus Christ
Our savior and our friend
He's the reason that we're here
Merry Christmas and Amen!

(The children recess out as the accompanist continues to play "Jingle Bells.")

The Night before Pageant

(From Sheryl J. Anderson, *The Twelve Plays of Christmas: Original Christian Dramas*, ©1999 by Judson Press. Reproduced by permission of Judson Press.)

(The CHOIR DIRECTOR, YOUTH LEADER, ELDER, and PASTOR stand before the altar, some pacing, all looking worried. The NARRATOR enters and looks them over; they do not see the Narrator. The Narrator takes a position to the side of the stage.)

NARRATOR: 'Twas the night before pageant
   And all through the chancel,
   The leaders were panicked,
   Wondering if they should cancel.
   A situation had come up
   That was really most dire:
   A bad winter flu
   Had laid low the whole choir.

CHOIR DIRECTOR: The Sunday before Christmas
   Is where the pageant belongs,
   But there cannot be a pageant
   Without our beautiful songs.

NARRATOR: The choir director announced
   In a rather hurt tone of voice,

CHOIR DIRECTOR: We will just have to cancel.
   There's really no choice.

NARRATOR: Now, that simple statement
   Put the youth leader in a tizzy.

YOUTH LEADER: I need to sit down.
   In fact, I feel dizzy.
   The children have practiced
   Since early November,
   They've learned where to stand
   And they finally remember
   Each one of their speeches
   And their Bible verses, too.
   If they don't perform,
   Who knows what they'll do.

NARRATOR: Then an Elder spoke up
With a sigh and a frown,

ELDER: If the whole choir's sick,
All attendance will be down.
With choir families home
Their kids won't be coming,
You'll have holes in your program.

YOUTH LEADER: Now I'm really bumming.
It just won't be Christmas
Without children all dressed
In their sweet little costumes.

PASTOR: The Lord's sent us a test.

NARRATOR: The leaders all nodded
At what the pastor had to say.
They could see he had a plan,
He would show them the way.

PASTOR: Each Sunday before Christmas
We put on a big show,
But it seems that this year
God is telling us no.
He must want us to celebrate
In a new and exciting way.
He must want us to think up
Something different to say.

ELDER: It had best be spectacular

NARRATOR: The elder said with a sad smile.

ELDER: Since people are busy,
We must make it worthwhile.
We can't expect them to give up
Games and parties and such
For a run-of-the-mill service,
That's asking too much.

NARRATOR: Then they all saw the pastor
Get that special twinkle in his eye,
The one he gets at council meetings
When a member pledges to tithe.

PASTOR: If we won't have our choir
And the children won't sing,
We can still have a service
And I know just the thing
That will cause the people's hearts
With Christmas joy to flower:
I will write my best sermon.
To fill up an hour.

NARRATOR: The leaders thought of his offer
A polite minute or so.
Considered it carefully,
Before saying,

LEADERS: No.

NARRATOR: Now, you can't blame the pastor
For seizing his chance,
But thank God we have leaders
In this circumstance.

YOUTH LEADER: So where does that leave us?

CHOIR LEADER: I'm afraid, high and dry.

PASTOR: Nothing else comes to mind.

ELDER: Oh, come on, we must try.

NARRATOR: And while they were thinking,
They heard a strange sound
From behind the altar
And they all turned around
To see the old sexton
Emerge from below or beneath,
With a dusty old crèche
And an evergreen wreath.

(The SEXTON emerges from behind the altar, carrying the items as described. He starts away from the group.)

SEXTON: Don't mean to disturb you,

NARRATOR: The sexton said humbly.

SEXTON: But you have a problem.

NARRATOR: The leaders nodded quite dumbly.
Lost in their thoughts,
They paid the old man no heed
Till he said to the pastor,

SEXTON: Seems to me what you need
Is to remember what the pageant
Has been all along.
It's not kids in bathrobes
Or old Latin songs.
It's to make folks remember
With a whisper, not a shout,
Make them stop, think of Jesus,
Whom the fuss is about.

PASTOR: You make it sound simple,
And that we admire,
But how do we do that
With no children or choir?

SEXTON: Just open the doors
So the people come in,
With just two or three,
The magic begins.
It's not about sermons,
Presents, or pageantry,
It's a Child
Who brings salvation for you and for me.
And that Babe is here with us
When we all stand as one.
Just unlock the front door,
And the hard part is done.

NARRATOR: The leaders realized in wonder
That wise sexton's words were all true.

PASTOR: On this Sunday evening,
That is just what we'll do.
We'll discard all the trappings
And try something new:
We will gather in faith
And that faith will see us through.

It will lead us in celebration
Of the most simple kind,
As we open our hearts
With the Lord's birth in mind.

(The Pastor shakes the Sexton's hand in thanks. The Sexton shrugs humbly, then walks away as the group looks after him in wonder.)

NARRATOR: And they heard him exclaim
As he shuffled from sight,

SEXTON: Now you all go on home,
I'm locking up for the night.

(The leaders all look at their watches, hurriedly bid each other good night, and exit in various directions.)

Oh, Come On, Emmanuel

(From Sheryl J. Anderson, *The Twelve Plays of Christmas: Original Christian Dramas*, ©1999 by Judson Press. Reproduced by permission of Judson Press.)

(A long line of people stretches across the playing area; the front of the line is out of sight, so we can't be sure where the line begins. Some people stand idly, staring off into space. Others read the paper or a book. One lady is knitting. FRED, at the end of the line, is working on a crossword puzzle.

PHYLLIS enters and walks by briskly, walking from the head to the end of the line. She glances up and notices the line, but keeps walking and exits. After a moment, she re-enters, studying the line from some distance. She gets a little closer. No one in the line reacts. Phyllis gets even closer, walking past Fred and several people in front of him. She stops, peering offstage, trying to see the beginning of the line. After a moment's thought, she steps back, even with Fred, trying her best to look casual.)

PHYLLIS: Is this the line?

FRED: *(Without looking up)* No, it's a work of modern art.

(Phyllis starts to get irritated, but then reconsiders, looking at the line again.)

PHYLLIS: I don't think I understand what the artist is trying to say.

(Fred looks up at her in surprise.)

FRED: It's the line, lady.

PHYLLIS: Oh, I got that part, I just wondered—

FRED: It's the line, lady. Just the line.

PHYLLIS: Oh. Oh, I see, you were making a joke before.

(Phyllis quickly steps into line behind Fred.)

PHYLLIS: You're a joker. I'll remember that and be ready next time.

FRED: That's okay, lady. There won't be a next time. I wouldn't want either of us to have to work that hard.

(Fred goes back to his crossword puzzle. Phyllis stands still a moment, then starts craning past Fred to try to see the front of the line. Fred tries to ignore her, but she's basically breathing down his neck. He clears his throat theatrically. Phyllis starts and steps back into her place in line.)

PHYLLIS: I was just trying to see . . .

FRED: It goes all the way up the street and around the corner.

PHYLLIS: So it's a long line.

FRED: As lines go.

PHYLLIS: Wow. That surprises me.

(Fred looks up from his crossword puzzle, looking at Phyllis a little more closely this time. She's still trying to peer around him, trying to study the line.)

FRED: It surprises you that this line is long?

PHYLLIS: Yes. A long line means a long wait, and most people just don't have the patience for that these days. But I guess you do.

FRED: *(With a tight smile)* I try to be patient. It's easier some times than others.

PHYLLIS: That's wonderful. I think patience is an admirable quality. I don't have much, myself.

FRED: Yet you're in line. And even further back than I am.

(Phyllis looks down at where she's standing, then tries to look toward the head of the line again, then shrugs.)

PHYLLIS: Well, some things are just worth waiting for.

FRED: Amen to that.

(Fred goes back to his crossword puzzle. Phyllis takes a deep breath.)

PHYLLIS: So. What are we waiting for?

(Fred looks up in surprise.)

FRED: You don't know what this line is for?

(Now the couple of people in front of Fred turn around to stare at Phyllis. She smiles and waves at them, trying not to be embarrassed.)

PHYLLIS: *(Low, to Fred)* Could you keep your voice down?

FRED: Excuse me, lady—

PHYLLIS: Phyllis.

(She puts her hand out to shake his, but he just looks at her hand uncomfortably.)

FRED: Phyllis, you've really caught me by surprise.

PHYLLIS: I can see that . . . ?

FRED: Fred.

PHYLLIS: Fred. Maybe you can surprise me now. And tell me what the line is for.

(JOAN, the lady in front of Fred, taps him on the shoulder.)

JOAN: She's just having a little fun with you.

FRED: You really think so? *(To Phyllis)* You're just pulling my leg?

JOAN: Of course she is. Everyone knows what the line is for.

PHYLLIS: I don't.

FRED: Then why did you get in the line?

PHYLLIS: Because it's so long. This many people lined up, they must be waiting for something important. A rock concert? A book signing? Free ice cream?

JOAN: This is not something to joke about.

PHYLLIS: *(Getting a little loud)* I'm not joking! What are we in line for?

(Now several of the people ahead of Joan and Fred turn around to stare. One of them, RUTH, hurries over.)

RUTH: She doesn't know?! An ignorant! I mean, an innocent. What a blessing. What an opportunity.

JOAN: Easy, Ruth. You're salivating.

RUTH: But I just get so excited whenever I get to tell someone what we're waiting for.

PHYLLIS: So tell me. Please. What are we waiting for?

FRED: We're waiting for Christmas.

RUTH: I wanted to tell her.

PHYLLIS: You're waiting for Christmas?

RUTH: Do you know about Christmas, dear? I'd be ever so happy to tell you all about it, to share the joy—

PHYLLIS: You're standing in line to wait for Christmas?

FRED: You seem to be having trouble with the concept.

PHYLLIS: Doesn't it strike you as a little strange?

Ruth: No. It's really not such a difficult concept. Christmas is a celebration—

Phyllis: Not the concept of Christmas. The concept of waiting for it.

Joan: But we have to wait for it. It only comes once a year, you know. Right? You do know that, don't you?

Phyllis: Yes, I know about Christmas.

Joan: Then you should understand that it's worth waiting for.

Phyllis: No, that part I don't get.

(Fred, Joan, and Ruth exchange a look of concern.)

Fred: Look, we don't want any trouble. If you're not interested in Christmas, you don't have to stay in the line.

Ruth: Yes, she does. With an attitude like hers, she needs all the Christmas she can get.

Phyllis: I have plenty of Christmas. Maybe even all the Christmas I need.

Ruth: *(With a little gasp)* Oh, that's just not possible.

Joan: You're probably one of those who figures, "I've done Christmas once, I don't need to do it again."

Phyllis: No, actually, I figure, I've done Christmas once and I'm still doing it and I'll be doing it forever.

Fred: I'm not sure I follow.

Phyllis: That's because you're following that long line of people ahead of you, Fred. A group of people who are content to stand still and let the world go by while they wait for Christmas.

Fred: We just don't want to miss it.

Phyllis: But you are missing it. Right now.

(Fred, Joan, and Ruth immediately check their watches. They compare watches, then turn back to Phyllis with frowns.)

Ruth: Don't scare us like that. Christmas is still quite a ways off.

(Ruth holds up her watch to prove her point. Phyllis waves it away.)

Phyllis: Christmas is right here.

(She points to the ground. Fred, Joan, and Ruth look attentively at the spot to which she points.)

RUTH: *(Loud whisper)* I don't see it.

PHYLLIS: *(Pointing to the sky)* And right here.

(The others follow her pointing again and shake their heads again.)

FRED: *(Loud whisper)* Looks like snow.

PHYLLIS: *(Pointing to her heart)* And right here.

(The other three look straight at her, bewildered.)

JOAN: You're Christmas?

PHYLLIS: I try to be.

RUTH: Oh, that's just vain and presumptuous.

PHYLLIS: I thought it was what God asks of us.

RUTH: Christmas is the celebration of the birth of the Savior. How can you possibly be Christmas?

PHYLLIS: Because I am constantly celebrating Jesus' birth.

FRED: That sounds tiring.

PHYLLIS: Not at all. It's invigorating. The Word is strong in me, so I'm strong. God's light has shined on me, so I shine. Christ lives in me, so I'm lively.

FRED: All year long?

PHYLLIS: Every moment of every day.

FRED: So Christmas is no big deal to you.

PHYLLIS: On the contrary. It is what I'm all about. It's my reason for living.

FRED: But if you carry it with you, you don't have to wait for it.

PHYLLIS: Exactly, Fred. Exactly.

FRED: *(As it sinks in)* Oh.

PHYLLIS: And if you feel you don't have Christmas in you every day, don't wait for it to come by again. Run to meet it. With your arms and your heart and your soul wide open. Embrace it. Absorb it. Live it and love it.

(Fred smiles at Phyllis, starting to get excited.)

FRED: And the joy of Christmas will be with me every day.

PHYLLIS: Because the promise of Christmas will be with you every day.

(Phyllis steps out of line and extends her hand to Fred. Fred starts to step out of line to join her, but Ruth and Joan grab him.)

JOAN: What are you doing?

RUTH: You're going to lose your place in line.

FRED: And gain the world.

(Fred steps out of line.)

JOAN: Don't blame us if you miss it.

PHYLLIS: Ladies, maybe you're the ones who are missing out.

(Phyllis starts to exit. She stops and looks back. Fred starts after her, then stops self-consciously. Phyllis gives him an encouraging smile and wave. Fred steps boldly out of line and starts after her.)

RUTH: Fred, what are you doing?

FRED: For starters, I'm going to meet Christmas halfway.

(He hurries after Phyllis and they exit together. Ruth and Joan look after them, shaking their heads in wonder, then turn around and resume waiting.)

While You Were Out

(From Sheryl J. Anderson, *The Twelve Plays of Christmas: Original Christian Dramas*, ©1999 by Judson Press. Reproduced by permission of Judson Press.)

(DONALD sits in his living room with his children, BUD and CONNIE. There are stacks of boxes around them, waiting to be wrapped, but the three just sit in stunned silence, staring into space. After a moment, DIANA enters, carrying shopping bags. She is in a tizzy.)

DIANA: I'm so sorry that I'm late, but I had to go to three stores to get the perfect sweater for Uncle George, and I had to ask for the manager at the jewelry store to get any help at all with our gift for Katie and—

(She stops, realizing for the first time that her husband and children are sitting motionless before her. She's surprised and then aggravated. Looks around at unwrapped boxes.)

Have the three of you just been sitting here since I left? How are we ever going to be ready for Christmas if I have to do everything myself? *(Starts to organize boxes)* Can't I count on the three of you to pitch in just a little? In the spirit of Christmas and all that?

(Donald stands up and indicates the couch.)

DONALD: Diana, I think you'd better sit down.

DIANA: What happened, Donald? You look so—well, so serious. Did someone die? Is someone sick? It must be someone on your side of the family, because no one on my side would have the nerve to get sick this time of year. *(Laughs nervously.)*

DONALD: No one's sick or dead, Diana.

(Diana puts down her packages and goes over to sit next to Donald.)

DIANA: Then what happened? The three of you look as though you'd seen a ghost.

BUD: Not exactly, Mom.

DIANA: What does that mean?

DONALD: Well, we did have a visitor. A most unexpected visitor.

CONNIE: *(Dazed)* A wonderful visitor.

BUD: Awesome, even.

DIANA: Did you offer cookies and eggnog? You know I like anyone who comes to the house to have cookies and eggnog this time of year, and I left a pitcher of eggnog and a plate of cookies in the refrigerator before I went out.

DONALD: Our visitor wasn't interested.

DIANA: Not interested? Those Christmas cookies were made from scratch with organic ingredients, and that eggnog didn't come out of a can either. And I grated the nutmeg myself!

CONNIE: Mom, I'm not sure the visitor *could* eat or drink.

DIANA: Oh, great. Six million things to do before Christmas and my family spends the afternoon entertaining some kind of nut. Is that what's happened to the three of you? You joined a cult while I was gone? I stand in line at Macy's for three hours to get Gramma the perfect china teapot and my family goes over to the Moonies.

BUD: Mom, our visitor was Christian. A real servant of Christ.

DIANA: And what am I? A temp for Christ? Who is making all the wise men's costumes for the pageant this year, thank you?

DONALD: No one is challenging your dedication, Diana. It's just that this fellow is an actual servant of Christ.

DIANA: Oh, so some missionary came by and hit you up for money to feed hungry children in Somewhere-or-other-stan. Did you tell him we sponsor three needy children on two different continents? And that I made them all little Christmas stockings with their difficult-to-pronounce little names cross-stitched on the top?

BUD: Mom, he was an angel.

DIANA: I'm sure he was, dear. Grumpy men don't get far in that profession.

DONALD: That's not what Bud means, dear. He means our guest was an actual angel.

DIANA: An actual angel. *(Looks from one to another.)* From heaven.

(Her family nods. Diana considers this a moment.)

DIANA: Donald, it's bad enough that you spiked the eggnog, but to give it to the children. Donald, they're underage!

CONNIE: Mom, we haven't had any eggnog. We had a—a visit from *(in amazement)* the angel Gabriel.

DIANA: Connie, this isn't funny.

DONALD: We agree. It's quite serious, Diana.

DIANA: Okay. Let's just say, for the moment, that I believe you. Let's say that the angel Gabriel really did come by our house for a visit this afternoon. What was so important that the Lord sent one of the holy angels to deliver a message to us in person?

DONALD: Christmas is coming.

(Diana rolls her eyes.)

DIANA: *(Sarcastically)* Well, you know, Donald, that had completely escaped my attention. I've just been running myself ragged baking and cooking and sewing and cleaning and shopping and who knows what else just for the fun of it. Is Christmas coming? How nice of the angel Gabriel to point that out.

CONNIE: No, Mom. Gabriel said that Christmas is coming, but we're so busy with our own ideas about it that we're not ready.

DIANA: Our own ideas? I've been chair of the Christmas Pot Luck Committee the last three years. I've organized the caroling to shut-ins this year. I know what Christmas is about! Who does this Gabriel think he is?

DONALD: I was suspicious too, dear, but—the more I think about it—

CONNIE: Gabriel is worried that we've gotten too caught up in things *about* Christmas to remember what Christmas really is.

DIANA: If Gabriel is so all-fired worried about our family, why did he come by when I wasn't home?

DONALD: Well, you were supposed to be home, dear.

DIANA: No, I was supposed to be out finishing the Christmas shopping. You three were supposed to be here wrapping and decorating and, heavenly visitor or no heavenly visitor, it would have been nice if you'd gotten something accomplished.

DONALD: Diana, it's Thursday night. The night we gather as a family for prayer and Bible study.

DIANA: And we'll do that again, right after Christmas. But right now, we need every minute we can find to get ready.

BUD: Gabriel said all we need to be ready for Christmas is a loving heart.

DIANA: Is that what you want under the tree Christmas morning, young man? A loving heart? That's fine by me, but I have a few computer games to return to the store if that's the case.

CONNIE: Mom, Gabriel said there's nothing wrong with exchanging gifts or any of the other holiday preparations we do, as long as they don't overwhelm us.

DIANA: Too late. I was overwhelmed by Thanksgiving.

CONNIE: Me, too. First finals, then my school concert, gifts to buy, and a new party dress. . . . But if things overwhelm us, they overwhelm the meaning of Christmas, too.

DIANA: According to Gabriel.

CONNIE: I wish you'd been here to talk to him, Mom. I was confused at first, but—he made a lot of sense.

DIANA: *(Frustrated)* But I enjoy Christmas!

DONALD: Sweetheart, you run yourself into the ground, race the clock, and usually wind up sick. That's not enjoying Christmas.

DIANA: But it's important to me that Christmas be perfect.

DONALD: A tiny baby born to save an entire sinful world forever. That's perfect, all by itself.

DIANA: *(Looking at him, puzzled)* This Gabriel really got to you, honey. You don't usually give the holiday a thought until Christmas Eve—when you rush around doing your shopping.

DONALD: Maybe I've been missing out on a lot—not just the exterior things, but preparing the *interior* too *(touching his heart)*, in here.

CONNIE: When I think about Mary giving birth to Jesus in a cold, dirty barn, well—worrying about finding the perfect party dress doesn't seem so important.

BUD: Yeah. Neither does a new hockey stick. Well—not as much anyway.

DIANA: But don't I make nice Christmases for the three of you?

DONALD: For us and everyone at church and everyone at work—yes, dear, you do. But Gabriel reminded us that you need to make a nice Christmas for yourself, too.

(Diana considers this a moment.)

DIANA: It would be nice to be happy and peaceful about Christmas. *(The others nod.)* And to be able to go to church Christmas Eve and think about something other than how tired I am. *(They nod again.)* And to be glad Christmas is here instead of hoping it will be over soon.

DONALD: It's possible, dear. We just need to simplify our plans a little.

DIANA: Like not making all three hundred of our Christmas cards by hand?

CONNIE: Right.

DIANA: And delegating a few of my duties at church to other members of my committees?

DONALD: Good.

DIANA: And making only two or three kinds of Christmas cookies instead of my usual thirteen or fourteen?

BUD: Let's not get carried away here.

DONALD: I'll pitch in with the Christmas errands so we'll *all* have time for getting our hearts ready for Jesus' coming.

DIANA: You make it all sound so simple.

CONNIE: I guess simple is what it's all about.

BUD: Yeah, it started in a stable, remember?

DIANA: No, I got caught up in the glitter and the noise and the nonsense. I need to get back to the stable. Think I can get there?

DONALD: Absolutely. Because we'll all go together.

(Donald and the children gather around Diana and hug her. She returns their hugs.)

DIANA: It was so nice of Gabriel to come by and talk to you. I'm so sorry I missed him. I should write him a nice note to say thank you. And maybe bake him a nice batch of cookies. Or maybe a fruitcake. Better yet, my famous seven-layer Christmas cake. Where did I put that recipe . . . ?

(She runs offstage. Donald and the children look at each other.)

DONALD: This may take a little more work than we thought. *(Running after her)* Diana! Wait!

BUD AND CONNIE: *(Running with him)* Mom!

(And they all run offstage.)

Live from Bethlehem

(From Sheryl J. Anderson, *The Twelve Plays of Christmas: Original Christian Dramas*, ©1999 by Judson Press. Reproduced by permission of Judson Press.)

(HARRY and LISA, a news anchor team, sit at their broadcast desk and address their "audience." They speak with the false cheeriness found on some television newscasts.)

HARRY: Good evening. I'm Harry Hathaway.

LISA: And I'm Lisa Van Heusen. Welcome to the Channel 3 News.

HARRY: Topping our broadcast tonight, strange goings-on in the town of Bethlehem.

LISA: That's right, Harry. Things have been chaotic there since the decree went forth from Caesar Augustus that all citizens were to return to the city of their fathers for a census. Guess lots of fathers came from Bethlehem, huh, Harry?

HARRY: Wish mine had, Lisa! I love Bethlehem this time of year.

(They share a little laugh, then snap back to announcing mode.)

LISA: But it's not just the census that's making life difficult for folks in Bethlehem tonight. For more on that, we go to our reporter, Ashley Ellis, who brings us this report, live from Bethlehem.

(On the other side of the playing area, a light reveals ASHLEY, dressed in a business suit and holding a microphone.)

Ashley, what can you tell us about the situation in Bethlehem tonight?

(Ashley puts her hand to her ear, adjusting her earpiece, as she begins to talk into the microphone.)

ASHLEY: Harry, Lisa, I am standing outside one of the famous inns of Bethlehem, inns known for their warm hospitality and their lovely accommodations. However, tonight, all the inns in Bethlehem are filled to capacity because of the heavy influx of people for the census. We have had reports that some people returning to Bethlehem have been forced to seek lodging in very unusual places—restaurants, shops—I was even told that there is a family staying in the stable behind this inn.

LISA: Is the stable still in use, Ashley?

ASHLEY: As best I can determine, yes. I have heard cattle lowing.

HARRY: Have you interviewed the family, Ashley?

ASHLEY: Not at the present time, Harry. We tried to get back there with our camera crew, but the stable and the whole area in front of the stable are packed with people.

LISA: Do they want to stay in the stable, too?

ASHLEY: No, apparently they are here to visit the family that is staying in the stable.

HARRY: If they have that many friends in Bethlehem, you'd think they'd have somewhere better to stay than a stable.

ASHLEY: That's what we're working to determine, Harry. Based on the people I have interviewed so far, most of the people crowding around the stable don't know the family inside.

HARRY: Do you have the identity of the family?

ASHLEY: Harry, I spoke with the innkeeper who gave them his permission to stay in the stable, and all he could tell me was that the husband is a carpenter from Nazareth and that his wife was pregnant and due to deliver at any moment. We have had word since we've been standing here that the wife has, in fact, brought forth a son, wrapped him in swaddling cloths, and laid him in the manger.

LISA: Boy, I bet their insurance company is going to have a field day with that one.

HARRY: So all the people who are there at the stable, Ashley—they heard about the baby and came to see him?

ASHLEY: Our investigation indicates that they have, in fact, come to worship him, Harry.

HARRY: Worship him?

ASHLEY: Yes, Harry, worship him. I have a witness to the situation here with me; perhaps he can clarify things for us a bit.

(Ashley waves someone into the spotlight with her. BOB, dressed as a biblical shepherd, complete with crook, hesitantly steps into the light.)

ASHLEY: Harry and Lisa, this is Bob Shepherd. Mr. Shepherd is one of the many people who have come to pay their respects at the stable. *(To Bob)* Thank you for agreeing to speak with us, Mr. Shepherd.

(Bob leans in self-consciously to make sure he's speaking into the microphone.)

BOB: Sure.

(He straightens up, smiles proudly, and turns to smile and nod at the unseen camera.)

ASHLEY: Can you tell us what brings you here tonight, Mr. Shepherd?

BOB: Well, yeah. The star.

ASHLEY: For those of you watching at home who did not see our special report at six, there is an incredibly large and bright star over the stable where this baby has been born. Experts are working to determine the exact cause of this astronomical oddity. So, Mr. Shepherd, you came to see the star?

BOB: Uh, no, I came to see the baby. I just followed the star to get here.

ASHLEY: So you're not from Bethlehem.

BOB: Yes, I am, but I was out in the fields, keeping watch over my sheep by night.

ASHLEY: You tend sheep?

BOB: *(Looking at her in disbelief)* No, I dress this way for fun.

ASHLEY: *(Pressing on)* And you were working—

BOB: And these angels appeared out of nowhere.

ASHLEY: Angels?

BOB: Yeah. This one angel came first, and the glory of the Lord shone round about him, and me and my buddies were sore afraid. I'm telling you, it was pretty scary! But the angel said, "Do not be afraid; for behold I bring you good news of a great joy which shall be for all the people; for today in the city of David there has been born for you a Savior, who is Christ the Lord."

ASHLEY: Did the angel offer any proof of this event?

BOB: You bet. He said, "This will be a sign for you; you will find a baby wrapped in cloths, and lying in a manger." And we thought that was pretty far-fetched and we weren't even that sure about this guy who said he was an angel, but suddenly, there appeared with this first angel guy a whole multitude of the heavenly host, praising God. You should have seen it. It would have blown you away.

ASHLEY: What statement did the heavenly host make?

BOB: It was something like, "Glory to God in the highest, And on earth peace among men with whom he is pleased."

ASHLEY: So what did you do then?

BOB: Well, we sat pretty still until the angels went back up into heaven, and then I said to my buddies, "Let us go straight to Bethlehem then, and see this thing that has happened which the Lord has made known to us."

ASHLEY: When you arrived, did you find the scene at the manger to be as the angels had foretold?

BOB: Pretty much. We came in haste and found Mary, that's the mother, and Joseph, that's the father, and the baby as he lay in the manger. And we told them what the angels had told us, and they seemed pretty cool with it. And we asked them if we could tell people, and they said sure, so that's why I agreed to talk to you.

ASHLEY: I find myself filled with wonder just hearing your story, Mr. Shepherd. Can you tell me how you feel having experienced it firsthand?

BOB: I'm still trying to take it all in, figure out what it might mean. But I glorify God and praise him that I was one of those chosen to witness this fulfillment of the prophecy.

ASHLEY: And which prophecy is that, Mr. Shepherd?

BOB: That the Messiah would come to us. You know, like the angels said, "There has been born for you a Savior, who is Christ the Lord."

ASHLEY: Have you been able to verify that this is, in fact, the baby that the angels spoke of?

BOB: Lady, I saw angels. They spoke to me. There's a star up there the size of the sun. And I'm filled with an amazing peace that I can't even begin to describe to you. What other kind of verification do you need?

ASHLEY: Has the baby done anything amazing?

BOB: Give him time, lady. Give him a little time.

(Bob walks away, leaving Ashley in the spotlight.)

ASHLEY: There you have it, Lisa and Harry. This breaking story where a group of shepherds is alleging that the Messiah has been born right here in Bethlehem. We're attempting to secure an interview with the family and get some pictures of the baby. We'll stay with the story and keep you up to date as it develops. For Channel 3 News, this is Ashley Ellis, live in Bethlehem.

(The light on Ashley goes out.)

LISA: Thank you, Ashley. Now, for more on that star that Ashley mentioned, let's go to our very own weather wizard, Windy Arrow. Windy, what can you tell us about this star?

*(A spotlight reveals WINDY, pert and perky in **a loud blazer.**)*

WINDY: Lisa and Harry, at first we thought that this so-called star was actually a great big ole pocket of swamp gas.

HARRY: Windy, Bethlehem is nowhere near a swamp.

WINDY: *(With a tight smile)* I know that, Harry. That's why we discarded that theory and decided that the star was actually a huge collection of ice crystals trapped in the lower atmosphere.

LISA: It's not very cold tonight.

WINDY: *(Still smiling)* I know that, Lisa. That's why we discarded that theory and decided that the star was actually a star.

LISA: A star?

WINDY: That's right. A star.

LISA: But witnesses have reported that it is making the area bright as day and that it's bigger than anything they've ever seen in the sky.

WINDY: Yup. It's quite a star, that I can confirm.

LISA: But can you explain it?

WINDY: Nope.

HARRY: You have no idea what could have caused this unusual star to appear over Bethlehem.

WINDY: I have no idea. I can't explain it at all.

HARRY: But you are working on it.

WINDY: Nope. I'm just waiting for it to go away. I have my hands full trying to predict the weather, Harry. When the heavens start coming down to earth with no warning, then I am out of my league. In fact, I start to get a little nervous and I—

(The light on Windy goes out abruptly. Lisa and Harry smile uncomfortably at the audience a moment.)

LISA: In an effort to bring you a slightly more reasonable explanation for today's events in Bethlehem, we have with us our political commentator, Dr. Edgar Cardigan, author of *The Only Book on Prophecy You'll Ever Need.*

(A light reveals DR. CARDIGAN, wearing a sweater with elbow patches and fidgeting with an unlit pipe.)

Thank you for joining us, Dr. Cardigan.

CARDIGAN: Thank you, Lisa.

LISA: Dr. Cardigan, I'm sure you're aware that there have been some interesting occurrences in Bethlehem today. Our viewers are very curious as to what it all might mean. Can you shed some light on this for us?

CARDIGAN: With that star up there, I can't see how anyone in Bethlehem needs more light.

(Lisa and Harry laugh politely. Cardigan doesn't even smile.)

HARRY: Surely there's a reasonable explanation for all this.

CARDIGAN: There's an explanation. How reasonable it is depends on your point of view.

LISA: *(Pressing on)* What's the explanation?

CARDIGAN: The Messiah has been born and all this has taken place that what was spoken by the Lord through the prophet might be fulfilled.

(Lisa and Harry sneak a nervous look at each other, then go back to smiling at Cardigan.) ·

LISA: Wow.

CARDIGAN: I'm sure that's how a lot of people feel.

HARRY: Doctor, are you saying that you believe the true Messiah is in a stable in Bethlehem?

CARDIGAN: I'm saying that the signs are all there. A star, a baby boy, angels, all coming together in the city of David at a time of great turmoil for our nation. . . . Based on this evidence, I am comfortable believing that this child could be the Messiah.

HARRY: Have you shared this information with anyone in the government?

CARDIGAN: No, Harry, because I don't think any of them are going to be too happy to hear it. Those of you who have read my book will remember that the government shall be on the shoulders of the Messiah, and he will be called Prince of Peace, among other things. I would say that means Prime Minister Herod and his cabinet will be looking for consulting jobs in the future.

LISA: Dr. Cardigan, have you had any contact with the family?

CARDIGAN: Not yet, Lisa, but I am planning to interview them later today. I want to confirm that the father is indeed of the house of David, that this is a virgin birth—

HARRY: Whoa, Doc. I don't know if we can say that on TV.

CARDIGAN: I will be monitoring the situation closely.

LISA: And we hope to have film at eleven.

HARRY: So, Doc, if this baby does turn out to be the Messiah, does that mean the world is about to end?

CARDIGAN: God only knows.

(Lisa and Harry smile bravely as this sinks in.)

LISA: Thank you, Dr. Cardigan.

(He nods and waves as his light goes out.)

Quite a story, huh, Harry?

HARRY: Absolutely amazing. I have a feeling we haven't heard the last of this kid.

LISA: Well, if he really is the Messiah, I hope he won't make the world end before this word from our sponsor.

(As they smile brightly, the lights go out.)

Echoes of Christmas

(From Sheryl J. Anderson, *The Twelve Plays of Christmas: Original Christian Dramas*, ©1999 by Judson Press. Reproduced by permission of Judson Press.)

This is a series of three choral readings, comprised of selected texts from the New American Standard Bible. A choral reading provides a dramatic opening to a worship service, particularly if the readers are not in front of the congregation (at the back of the sanctuary, in the choir loft, etc.) and the congregation concentrates on the words, not the performers. You might consider doing these three on consecutive Sundays or incorporating all three into one worship service, using one as an opening, one as an offertory, and one as a closing.

Echoes of the Prophecy

READER 1:   For a child will be born to us

READER 2:   Behold, the virgin shall be with child, and shall bear a son

READER 3:   Whoever receives this child in My name receives Me

READER 4:   You must be born again

READER 1:   A son will be given to us

READER 2:   And this will be a sign for you

READER 4:   The Son of Man is Lord of the Sabbath

READER 3:   This is my beloved Son, in whom I am well pleased

READER 1:   And the government will rest on His shoulders

READER 4:   And I saw a new heaven and a new earth

READER 3:   Did you not know that I had to be in My father's house?

READER 2:   You shall receive power when the Holy Spirit has come upon you; and you shall be My witnesses

READER 1:   And His name will be called

READER 4:   They shall call his name Immanuel, which means "God with us"

READER 1:   Wonderful Counselor

READER 3:   Why do you call me "Lord, Lord" and not do what I say?

READER 1:   Mighty God

READER 2:   He went to Jesus and said, "Hail, Rabbi!"

READER 1:   Eternal Father

READER 4:   And he replied, "Say it, Teacher"

READER 1:   Prince of Peace

READER 2:   Then what shall I do with Him whom you call the king of the Jews?

READER 1:   There will be no end to the increase of His government

READER 4:   The kingdom of the world has become the kingdom of our Lord

READER 2:   To Him who sits on the throne, and to the Lamb, be blessing and honor and glory and dominion forever and ever

READER 3:   If you ask me anything in My name, I will do it

READER 1:   Or of peace

READER 2:   Peace I leave with you; My peace I give to you

READER 3:   These things I have spoken to you, that in Me you may have peace

READER 4:   Go in peace. Serve the Lord

READER 1:   On the throne of David and over his kingdom

READER 2:   Today in the city of David there has been born for you a Savior

READER 4:   For thine is the kingdom

READER 3:   In My Father's house are many dwelling places

READER 1:   To establish it and to uphold it

READER 2:   Go and proclaim everywhere the kingdom of God

READER 3:   For this I have been born, and for this I have come into the world, to bear witness to the truth

READER 4:   Go into all the world and preach the gospel to all creation

READER 1:   With justice and righteousness

READER 2:   I will put my Spirit upon Him, and he shall proclaim justice to the Gentiles

READER 4:   Then the righteous will shine forth as the sun in the kingdom of their Father

READER 3:   The righteous shall live by faith

READER 1:   From then on and forevermore

READER 4:   World without end

READER 3:   I am the Alpha and the Omega

READER 2:   Thus it is written

READER 1:   Amen

READER 4:   So shall it be

READER 2:   Amen

READER 1:   He who has an ear, let him hear

READER 3:   Amen

READER 2:   This is the word of the Lord

READER 4:   Amen

Scripture references, in order of occurrence:
Isaiah 8:6-7; Matthew 1:23, 18:5; John 3:7; Luke 2:12; Matthew 12:8, 3:7; Revelation 21:1; Luke 2:49; Acts 1:8; Isaiah 7:14; Luke 6:46; Matthew 26:49, 13:1; Mark 5:12; Revelation 11:15, 5:13; John 14:14, 14:27, 16:33; James 2:16; Luke 2:11; Matthew 6:13; John 14:2; Luke 8:60; John 18:37; Mark 16:15; Matthew 12:18, 13:43; Romans 1:17; Revelation 22:13, 2:7

Echoes of the Announcement

READER 1: Hail, favored one! The Lord is with you

READER 2: Blessed is He who comes in the name of the Lord

READER 3: And on earth peace among men with whom He is pleased

READER 4: I am not alone, because the Father is with me

READER 1: Do not be afraid, Mary; for you have found favor with God

READER 4: Take courage; it is I, do not be afraid

READER 3: For behold, I bring you good news of a great joy

READER 2: Be strong in the Lord, and in the strength of His might

READER 1: And behold, you will conceive in your womb and bear a son

READER 2: Therefore, He had to be made like His brethren in all things

READER 4: For the Son of Man is going to be delivered into the hands of men

READER 3: Be on the alert, for you do not know which day your Lord is coming

READER 1: And you shall name Him Jesus

READER 2: Hallowed be Thy name

READER 3: At the name of Jesus every knee should bow

READER 4: I am the light of the world

READER 1: He will be great

READER 3: Then He arose, and rebuked the winds and the seas; and it became perfectly calm

READER 4: I say to you, rise, take up your pallet and go home

READER 2: This is the one who baptizes in the Holy Spirit

READER 1: And will be called the Son of the Most High

READER 4: Who do the multitudes say that I am?

READER 3: He who has the Son has the life

READER 2: No one knows the Son, except the Father

READER 1: And the Lord God will give Him the throne of His father David

READER 3: I am the root and the offspring of David, the bright morning star

READER 2: Lord, have mercy on us, Son of David!

READER 4: If David then called him "lord," how is He his son?

READER 1: And He will reign over the house of Jacob forever

READER 2: I am the God of Abraham, and the God of Isaac, and the God of Jacob

READER 3: The Deliverer will come from Zion, He will remove ungodliness from Jacob

READER 4: To Him who sits on the throne, and to the Lamb, be blessing and honor and glory and dominion forever and ever

READER 1: And His kingdom will have no end

READER 3: Behold, I am alive forevermore

READER 2: We receive a kingdom which cannot be shaken

READER 4: My kingdom is not of this world

READER 1: For nothing will be impossible with God

READER 3: Faith is the assurance of things hoped for, the conviction of things not seen

READER 4: All things are possible to him who believes

READER 2: Your faith has made you well

READER 1: Amen

READER 3: For Thine is the kingdom

READER 2: Amen

READER 4: And the power and the glory

READER 3: Amen

READER 2: Forever and ever

READER 4: Amen

Scripture references in order of occurrence:
Luke 1:28–33; Matthew 21:9; Luke 2:14; John 8:16; Matthew 14:27; Luke 2:10; Ephesians 6:10; Hebrews 2:17; Mark 9:31; Matthew 24:42; Luke 11:2; Philippians 2:10; John 8:12; Matthew 8:26; Mark 2:9; John 1:33; Luke 8:18; John 5:12; Matthew 11:27; Revelations 22:16; Matthew 9:27; Luke 20:44; Mark 12:26; Romans 11:26; Revelation 5:13, 1:18; Hebrews 12:28; John 18:36; Hebrews 11:1; Mark 9:23; Luke 17:19

Echoes of the Acceptance

READER 1: My soul exalts the Lord

READER 2: If these become silent, the stones will cry out

READER 3: Blessed be the Lord God of Israel

READER 4: I praise Thee, O Father, Lord of heaven and earth

READER 1: And my spirit has rejoiced in God my Savior

READER 3: Rejoice in the Lord always; again I will say, rejoice!

READER 4: We exult in hope of the glory of God

READER 2: Rejoice, and be glad, for your reward in heaven is great

READER 1: For He has had regard for the humble state of his bondslave

READER 3: There is neither Jew nor Greek, there is neither slave nor free man

READER 2: And the slave does not remain in the house forever; the son does remain forever

READER 4: But the greatest among you shall be your servant

READER 1: For behold, from this time on all generations will count me blessed

READER 3: Blessed among women are you, and blessed is the fruit of your womb!

READER 4: And Mary treasured up all these things, pondering them in her heart

READER 2: Blessed are the pure in heart, for they shall see God

READER 1: For the Mighty One has done great things for me

READER 4: We love, because He first loved us

READER 2: For it is God who is at work in you, both to will and to work for His good pleasure

READER 3: He is not the God of the dead, but of the living; for all live to Him

READER 1: And holy is His name

READER 2: Blessed is He who comes in the name of the Lord

READER 3: I have come in my Father's name

READER 4: For where two or three have gathered together in My name, there I am in their midst

READER 1: And His mercy is upon generation after generation toward those who fear Him

READER 3: You are not far from the kingdom of God

READER 2: All things for which you pray and ask, believe that you have received them, and they shall be granted you

READER 4: How much more shall your Heavenly Father give the Holy Spirit to those who ask Him?

READER 1: He has done mighty things with His arm

READER 4: I will destroy this temple made with hands, and in three days I will build another made without hands

READER 3: Every tree that does not bear good fruit is cut down and thrown into the fire

READER 2: Yet not what I will, but what Thou wilt

READER 1: He has scattered those who were proud in the thoughts of their heart

READER 3: Woe to you when all men speak well of you, for in the same way their fathers used to treat the false prophets

READER 4: Beware of practicing your righteousness before men to be noticed by them

READER 2: You shall love your neighbor as yourself

READER 1: He has brought rulers down from their thrones

READER 4: No one can serve two masters

READER 2: For what is a man profited if he gains the whole world, and loses . . . himself?

READER 3: Seek first His kingdom and His righteousness

READER 1: And has exalted those who were humble

READER 2: Thus the last shall be first, and the first last

READER 3: Let us therefore draw near with confidence to the throne of grace

READER 4: For all shall know Me, from the least to the greatest of them

READER 1: He has filled the hungry with good things

READER 3: Take, eat; this is My body

READER 4: Blessed are you who hunger now, for you shall be satisfied

READER 2: Do not be anxious then, saying, "What shall we eat?" or "What shall we drink?"

READER 1: And sent away the rich empty-handed

READER 3: Woe to you who are rich, for you are receiving your comfort in full

READER 4:   Do not lay up for yourselves treasures upon earth, where moth and rust destroy, and where thieves break in and steal

READER 2:   It is easier for a camel to go through the eye of a needle than for a rich man to enter the kingdom of God

READER 1:   He has given help to Israel His servant, in remembrance of His mercy

READER 4:   And I saw the holy city, new Jerusalem, coming down out of heaven from God

READER 2:   Do not think that I came to abolish the Law or the Prophets

READER 3:   A light of revelation to the Gentiles, and the glory of Thy people Israel

READER 1:   As He spoke to our fathers, To Abraham and his offspring forever

READER 2:   For when God made the promise to Abraham, since He could swear by no one greater, He swore by Himself

READER 3:   For this is the covenant that I will make with the house of Israel after those days, says the Lord

READER 4:   Jesus Christ is the same yesterday and today, yes and forever

READER 1:   Amen

READER 3:   Glory be to the Father

READER 2:   Amen

READER 4:   And to the Son

READER 3:   Amen

READER 2:   And to the Holy Ghost

READER 4:   Amen

Scripture references, in order of occurrence:
Luke 1:46–55, 19:40, 1:68; Matthew 11:25; Philippians 4:4; Romans 5:2; Matthew 5:12; Galatians 3:28; John 8:35; Matthew 20:26; Luke 5:2; Matthew 5:12; 1 John 4:19; Philippians 2:13; Luke 20:38; Mark 11:9; John 5:43; Matthew 18:20; Mark 12:34, 11:24; Luke 11:13; Mark 14:58; Matthew 3:10; Mark 14:36; Luke 6:23; Matthew 6:1, 5:43, 6:24; Luke 9:25; Matthew 6:33, 19:30; Hebrews 4:16, 8:11; Matthew 26:26; Luke 6:21; Matthew 6:31; Luke 6:24; Matthew 6:19; Matthew 19:23; Revelation 21:2; Matthew 5:17; Luke 2:32; Hebrews 6:3, 8:10, 13:0

Hanging on the Tree

(From Sheryl J. Anderson, *The Twelve Plays of Christmas: Original Christian Dramas*, ©1999 by Judson Press. Reproduced by permission of Judson Press.)

(The setting is a living room with an undecorated Christmas tree prominently displayed. There are a couple of boxes marked CHRISTMAS DECORATIONS on the floor near the tree. A toolbox sits next to them. MARK enters with a strand of lights, trying to stay patient while he tries to untangle them. There is a knock at the front door and Mark crosses to open it, revealing his friend RICK.)

MARK: Hey, Rick, come on in.

RICK: Sorry to bother you, Mark. You seem kinda tied up.

MARK: No, just trying to lighten up.

(They exchange high fives and Rick enters.)

RICK: Looks like we're doing the same thing this afternoon. I'm putting up Christmas decorations, too.

MARK: Yeah, my team doesn't stand a chance of making it to the playoffs, so I figured that was God's way of telling me to turn off the TV and get ready for Christmas.

RICK: Well, I don't know what God was trying to tell me, but I just knocked the head off Rudolph while I was trying to hoist him onto the roof. Can I borrow some duct tape?

MARK: Sure. It's over there in my toolbox.

(Mark points and Rick walks over to the toolbox.)

So Rudolph's head came off, huh?

RICK: Yeah. I'm actually surprised it didn't happen long before this. Rudolph dates back to before the kids were born. I'd like to get rid of him, but the rest of the family's being sentimental about it.

(Rick finds the duct tape.)

MARK: Christmas brings that out in people.

RICK: Speaking of sentimental—

(He reaches into one of the boxes of Christmas decorations and pulls out an old phone.)

RICK: Couldn't bear to part with an old phone, buddy? That's beyond senti-mental. That's serious pack rat stuff.

MARK: It's not just a broken phone.

RICK: No? You use it as a paperweight, too?

MARK: It's a Christmas decoration.

RICK: A what?

MARK: A Christmas decoration. We're going to put it on the tree.

RICK: What bizarre decorating magazine is your wife subscribing to now?

MARK: The phone represents all the time we've wasted and all the people we've hurt with idle gossip.

RICK: And you're going to put it on your Christmas tree.

MARK: Right.

RICK: Go on.

MARK: That's all there is to it.

RICK: Come on, Mark, I'm waiting for the punch line.

MARK: There is no punch line, Rick.

RICK: Then it's not a very good joke.

MARK: It's not a joke at all.

RICK: Okay, say I buy this whole thing about the phone being a symbol.

MARK: Okay.

RICK: Why would you want to hang a symbol of something so dark and depress-ing on your Christmas tree?

MARK: Where else should I hang it?

RICK: Oh, I don't know. An art gallery, the bathroom wall, the trash can—but not your Christmas tree!

MARK: Why not?

RICK: Because a Christmas tree is a pretty thing, a happy thing. How can you want to ruin it with this big clunky symbol of something painful?

MARK: Because that's what Christmas trees are for.

RICK: No. No. Christmas trees are to symbolize the eternal freshness of God's promise to us. You know, the whole evergreen thing. Now, that's a nice symbol. A happy symbol.

MARK: Okay, that's the tree itself. What about the ornaments?

RICK: Again, pretty and joyous. Angels and snowmen and reindeer and stars. Not phones and—

(Rick reaches randomly into a box and pulls out a little dead plant in a small pot.)

A dead plant.

MARK: A dead mustard plant, actually. To remind us of the opportunities God has given us that we have ignored or run away from.

RICK: That's just lovely. I'm feeling more Christmas spirit by the minute. And, of course, what tree would be complete without—

(Rick reaches in again and lifts out a bag of candy.)

A bag of candy. Oh, okay. This is better. A bag of candy is happy.

MARK: It's a symbol of gluttony and selfishness.

RICK: Oh, man, I am not getting through to you, am I?

(Rick drops everything back in the boxes. Mark puts down the lights and comes over to the boxes with Rick.)

MARK: I hear what you're saying, Rick, and I don't disagree. I just don't think you're considering the whole picture. A Christmas tree symbolizes more than God's eternal love.

RICK: Right. According to you, it apparently also symbolizes a lot of very deeply rooted emotional problems. Maybe we can find a little therapist for you to put on top of the tree instead of an angel.

MARK: Rick, when you look at a Christmas tree, what do you see?

RICK: Am I looking at your tree or mine?

MARK: Any tree.

RICK: I see light and hope and joy and the promise of salvation.

MARK: And what do you have to do to get those things?

RICK: I have to have faith and repent of my sins.

MARK: And how do you repent?

RICK: I present my sins to God and I say, "I'm sorry and I'll try very hard not to do that anymore."

MARK: Right.

RICK: Right. Okay, now that we've reviewed our confirmation lessons, what's that got to do with your morbid approach to decorating a Christmas tree?

MARK: When I decorate my tree, I'm presenting my sins to God and saying, "I'm sorry."

RICK: But Christmas isn't about repentance. Christmas is about a new beginning.

MARK: And how better to begin than with a contrite heart?

RICK: Christmas is supposed to be joyous.

MARK: And with every sin I present, I'm joyous because I know that sin is forgiven.

RICK: But Christmas isn't about sin!

MARK: You're right. Christmas is about Christ. But doesn't a lot of our relationship with him deal with our sins?

(Rick has to think about that one for a moment.)

Rick, it gives me great peace and happiness at Christmas to be able to hang all my sins on the tree. That way, come Easter, when Christ is hanging on the tree because of my sins, I know I've been with him every step of the way. Which means I'm making the whole journey with him. From Christmas to Easter to heaven, hand in hand, every inch of the way.

RICK: Okay now. Once you explain it, it makes sense.

MARK: I knew you'd understand.

RICK: Oh, yeah, I understand. I just have one more question.

MARK: Sure. Ask away.

RICK: I have this beautiful jacket my wife says is ugly as sin. Want to hang it on your tree? My contribution?

(Mark shakes his head at Rick.)

The Big One

(From Sheryl J. Anderson, *The Twelve Plays of Christmas: Original Christian Dramas,* ©1999 by Judson Press. Reproduced by permission of Judson Press.)

(The setting is a locker room. Several team members in gym attire are stretching out or toweling off. GABE and MIKE sit next to each other on a bench, lacing up their shoes.)

GABE: I gotta tell you, Mike, I don't know how much longer I can wait. I've been training and training and I know I'm ready. I can do it. I just need the chance.

MIKE: Come on, Gabe, you know only one guy can make that call.

GABE: But he's seen me play, he knows I'm good. Fast, confident, and I blow them away. I want this bad, Mike.

MIKE: I know you do, Gabe, and I think you're the go-to guy. You've never dropped the ball on us, but I'm not in charge of the roster. You gotta have faith, man. Your moment is coming.

(A WHISTLE blows and everyone in the locker room snaps to attention. They wait nervously as the COACH enters, carrying a clipboard.)

COACH: All right, listen up.

ALL: Yes, Coach!

COACH: And go ahead and sit down. This could take a while.

(They all sit down. The Coach consults his clipboard and takes a deep breath before beginning.)

Okay, first of all, I want to say that I'm really pleased with how the training's going. Everyone's really working hard, giving their all, really committing to the program.

(The members of the team congratulate each other.)

You're a terrific team and I appreciate the way you all pull together.

MIKE: You bring out the best in us, Coach.

(Everyone nods in agreement. Coach shrugs it off.)

COACH: You came to me with the fire already in you. I'm just helping you refine it. But . . .

MIKE: Uh-oh. But what, Coach?

COACH: The big guy has made a change in the schedule. And it's a major shakeup. I know we were planning on our regular appearances to prophets and that kind of thing, but it's time for the Big One.

(The team gasps and whispers among themselves. Gabe grabs Mike's arm in excitement.)

GABE: The Big One. Mike, did you hear that?

MIKE: I sure did.

COACH: You know the big guy does things in his own time, and he has decided it's time for his son to put in an appearance.

(Gabe can't take the excitement anymore. He jumps to his feet.)

GABE: Send me, Coach. Send me. I can do it. I'm ready.

COACH: Ready for what, Gabe?

GABE: For anything you ask of me, Coach. I want to be a part of this.

COACH: We're all a part of it, Gabe.

GABE: But I want to be a special part of it. I want to tell the whole world that the son is on his way.

(Coach shakes his head. Gabe deflates.)

COACH: I can't let you do that, Gabe.

GABE: But, Coach, I've got the wings, I've got the blinding light, I've got what it takes.

COACH: I know you do, Gabe, and I think you're the guy for the job.

GABE: But you just said—

COACH: I said you can't tell the whole world.

GABE: I don't think I understand.

COACH: You can't tell the whole world, but you can tell one person.

GABE: Big news like this, maybe the biggest news ever, and I can only tell one person?

COACH: That's the game plan.

MIKE: Kind of odd. *(Coach looks at him with eyebrows raised. Mike adds hastily)* Not that I'm questioning the game plan.

GABE: Who's the one person who gets to know the news? A king? A prophet?

COACH: A young woman in Nazareth.

GABE: What's she got to do with this?

COACH: She's going to bear the son.

(There is a moment of stunned silence.)

MIKE: The big guy is going to have his son be born? As in, born a human?

COACH: Exactly.

MIKE: Wow. That's taking a risk.

COACH: I think the boss knows what he's doing.

MIKE: True. We're always victorious when we stick to his game plans.

GABE: So does this lady in Nazareth know anything about this?

COACH: Not a thing.

GABE: Oh, man, this is poor Zacharias all over again.

COACH: Poor Zacharias? He's a very blessed man, Gabe. He and his wife are going to raise the child who will be the ultimate messenger of God.

MIKE: Not that we're all that shabby.

GABE: But he was struck dumb. And he's an experienced servant of the Lord. This news is a million times more important than the news I gave him, and I'm going to give it you a young woman who isn't expecting to be expecting?

COACH: That's right.

GABE: Shouldn't we break it to her gently? Maybe I appear to her in a dream or two, leave some divine signs around her house . . . ?

COACH: *(Shaking his head)* That's not how the big guy wants it to happen, Gabe.

GABE: So I'm going to go appear before her in the whole divine apparition regalia and lay this on her? That's a lot for a person to absorb. It's a lot for me to absorb. What if she doesn't believe me?

COACH: Gabe, she'll believe you. She was picked for this mission because she is a woman of extraordinary and exquisite faith. And you were picked for this mission because you are sincere and powerful and not quite as scary as Mike can be.

(Mike shrugs apologetically.)

GABE: So what do I tell her?

COACH: Here. I drafted something for you.

(Coach hands Gabe a piece of paper from the clipboard.)

GABE: *(Reading)* "Hail, favored one! The Lord is with you. Do not be afraid, Mary—" *(to Coach)* You think she might be afraid?

COACH: It might take her a few moments to get over your sudden appearance.

GABE: Yeah, I can be a little breathtaking. *(Reading again)* "Do not be afraid, Mary; for you have found favor with God. And behold, you will conceive in your womb, and bear a son—" *(to Coach)* How's that going to happen?

COACH: I've got it covered. I'll explain it to you later. Keep reading.

GABE: *(Reading)* "And you shall name him Jesus."

MIKE: Jesus. That's a great name.

COACH: For a great kid.

GABE: *(Reading)* "He will be great, and will be called the Son of the Most High; and the Lord God will give him the throne of his father David; and he will reign over the house of Jacob forever; and his kingdom will have no end."

(The team stands and applauds. Gabe looks at Coach in wonder.)

COACH: Sounds terrific, Gabe.

GABE: Coach, I can't tell you how much this means to me.

COACH: Just do a good job while you're down there, kiddo, and that'll be all the thanks I need.

GABE: I'll give it everything I've got, Coach, and everything I am.

COACH: I knew I could count on you. So let's get you suited up.

GABE: Now?

COACH: You said you were ready.

GABE: I am, I just didn't expect it all to happen so soon.

COACH: It's not sudden, Gabe. The whole world is waiting.

(Mike and the other team members cheer as Coach leads Gabe out.)

Tidings of Comfort and Joy

(From Sheryl J. Anderson, *The Twelve Plays of Christmas: Original Christian Dramas,* ©1999 by Judson Press. Reproduced by permission of Judson Press.)

(The front yard of a suburban home. CAROLERS enter and line up in the front yard as they sing "Silent Night." As they finish the song, DAVE and JOYCE come out of their house and stand on the front step. When the song is finished, Dave and Joyce applaud. The leader of the carolers, LYNN, steps forward.)

LYNN: Thank you very much.

(She turns to her carolers, gives them the downbeat, and they begin to sing.)

CAROLERS: *(Singing)* We wish you a happy Easter, we wish you a happy Easter, we wish you a happy—

DAVE: Excuse me.

(The carolers stop uncertainly. Lynn turns to look at Dave.)

LYNN: Would you prefer we do it in a different key so you can sing along?

DAVE: No, no, you sound fine on your own. It's just—I could have sworn you were singing "We wish you a happy Easter."

LYNN: That's right.

JOYCE: But it's Christmas.

LYNN: That's right.

JOYCE: So, shouldn't you be singing Christmas songs?

LYNN: It is a Christmas song.

DAVE: It's usually a Christmas song, but not the way you're singing it.

LYNN: What's wrong with the way we're singing it?

DAVE: You're saying "Easter" instead of "Christmas"!

LYNN: Right.

DAVE: *(Waiting for her to recognize her error)* So . . . ?

LYNN: *(Unruffled)* So?

JOYCE: *(To Dave)* I don't think we're getting through to her, Dave. Maybe we should go back inside. It's cold out here.

DAVE: Of course it's cold. It's December. It's Christmas.

44

LYNN: Pardon me, sir, but you seem quite upset.

DAVE: And you can't imagine why?

LYNN: Perhaps another song would help.

(She gives the carolers another downbeat and they sing.)

CAROLERS: *(Singing)* God rest you merry, gentlemen, let nothing you dismay. Remember, Christ our Savior was raised on Easter Day—

DAVE: *(Incensed)* Would you stop with the Easter stuff?

(The carolers stop, looking at Dave like he's crazy.)

LYNN: Nope. Sorry. Can't do that.

JOYCE: You can't stop singing about Easter?

LYNN: Nope.

JOYCE: Why not?

LYNN: Because you can't have one without the other.

JOYCE: Can't have Easter without singing?

LYNN: Nope. Can't have Christmas without Easter.

DAVE: I don't know where you're from, young lady, or what kind of bizarre cult you belong to, but around here, we know the difference between Christmas and Easter.

LYNN: Oh, I know the difference.

DAVE: Can't tell, judging by your songs.

LYNN: All I'm saying is, you can't have Christmas without Easter.

JOYCE: So you probably think you can't have Easter without Christmas, either.

LYNN: That's exactly right. Now you're following us.

DAVE: We're not following you anywhere because the only place you're going is out of our yard. Can't have Christmas without Easter. Indeed . . .

(Dave starts to lead Joyce into the house.)

LYNN: Just think about it for a minute. Why does Christmas make you happy?

(Joyce stops and turns around to answer. Dave tugs on her arm.)

DAVE: Don't get sucked into this, Joyce. This is how these cults work. They wear you down with their nonsense until you start to think they sound reasonable.

JOYCE: But Dave, she asked a fair question. If I give good Christian witness in my answer, maybe I can help turn her away from her confusion.

DAVE: Okay. But be careful.

(Both Dave and Joyce turn back to face Lynn and the carolers.)

JOYCE: Christmas makes me happy because it reminds me of the birth of my Lord and Savior, Jesus Christ.

LYNN: And how did he become your Lord and Savior, ma'am?

JOYCE: He died on the cross for all our sins.

LYNN: And that happened on . . .

(Joyce glances at Dave a little nervously. Dave is watching Lynn intently now.)

JOYCE: Easter?

LYNN: Exactly.

JOYCE: Oh, dear. I think I'm beginning to get her point.

DAVE: Christmas and Easter are still two completely different days. Two completely different events. Birth and death. The beginning and the end.

LYNN: The Alpha and the Omega. Isn't part of the joy of Christ's birth knowing that he's going to die on the cross for us? Isn't part of the triumph of Easter knowing that this was the Savior who was born among us as a tiny child? There is no beginning, there is no end, except in God. God encompasses all things and makes them one. Even Christmas and Easter.

JOYCE: Oh, Dave. I'm afraid she's right.

DAVE: There's no need to be afraid, Joyce.

JOYCE: But she's right, isn't she?

DAVE: Yes, dear, I think she is.

JOYCE: So what are we going to do about it?

DAVE: There's only one thing we can do, dear.

(Dave leads Joyce off the front steps and over to the carolers. Dave gives the downbeat and everyone sings.)

ALL: *(Singing)* We wish you a happy Easter, we wish you a happy Easter, we wish you a happy Easter, Merry Christmas, too.

Traveling with Reservations

(From Sheryl J. Anderson, *The Twelve Plays of Christmas: Original Christian Dramas,* ©1999 by Judson Press. Reproduced by permission of Judson Press.)

(The MANAGER stands behind the front counter of a small motel, leafing through a magazine. After a moment, the BELL RINGS as the front door opens. JOE enters, rather windblown. The Manager looks up and smiles automatically.)

MANAGER: Good evening and welcome to the Inn on the Square.

JOE: Thank you very much.

MANAGER: Still windy out, huh?

(Joe tries to smooth his hair down, then winds up running his hand nervously through his hair instead.)

JOE: Part wind, part nerves. Bad habit.

(The Manager holds up his hand.)

MANAGER: Not so bad. I chew my fingernails.

JOE: I may take that up, too.

MANAGER: Little stressed, sir?

JOE: My wife's expecting.

MANAGER: Ah, I see. Must be the first one. *(Joe nods.)* I remember the feeling. Like waiting for eternity to roll by. I finally got to the point where I said, "Just bring it on. I can handle it."

JOE: And did you handle it?

MANAGER: No. But I survived it. And my kids still talk to me. And my wife still talks to me. Most days. So I figure I did okay. You will, too. *(Opening the ledger)* You have reservations?

JOE: Brother, do I. I'm not sure I'm going to be a good father and I certainly wasn't expecting to be a father this soon and it's all out of my hands anyway, and maybe that's why I feel so out of control—

MANAGER: Whoa, whoa, buddy. I meant, you have reservations here at my motel?

JOE: Oh. No. I don't. I guess you could say I'm here on a wing and a prayer.

(The Manager looks at Joe in disbelief and flips the ledger closed.)

MANAGER: I don't know that I can help you.

JOE: But you have to help me. I've tried every other place in town.

MANAGER: I'm sure you have. Whole town is booked solid. It's the census.

JOE: Well, I'm here for the census, too.

MANAGER: Being here for the census doesn't entitle you to a room, Mr.—

JOE: Davidson. Joe Davidson.

MANAGER: Mr. Davidson. You should have made a reservation when you first got the census notice.

JOE: I've had a lot on my mind.

MANAGER: I can imagine.

JOE: I doubt that.

MANAGER: Listen, Mr. Davidson, I told you I'm sympathetic to your baby anxiety, but trust me—you are not the first guy to go through this.

JOE: Actually, I think I am. My situation is somewhat . . . unique.

MANAGER: Every new dad feels that way. With my first kid, I was convinced I was the only husband in the world whose wife craved garlic mashed potatoes at three in the morning. With the second kid, she got charley horses every night and would kick so hard she'd knock me out of the bed. Since the last three kids, I've been so tired that my memory's shot, but I'm sure there was something with each one of them, too.

JOE: So how did you get through it?

MANAGER: Love.

JOE: Love?

MANAGER: Uh-huh.

JOE: For whom?

MANAGER: My wife. My kids. And the good Lord who gave them all to me.

JOE: That's it? Love got you through it?

MANAGER: And faith. I figure a God who loves me enough to give me such a wonderful family didn't do it to make me crazy or broke or old before my time, even though I usually feel at least two of those. I figure if God has enough faith in me to entrust me with these treasures, I can have enough faith in God to believe that he will help me take care of them.

JOE: Well, I know this sounds vain, but I do know that God must think I'm special.

MANAGER: Nothing vain about that, Mr. Davidson. Just shows you're a man with a living faith. It's good to remember that God thinks we're special.

JOE: I mean, really special.

MANAGER: Absolutely! As special as humanly possible. You know, I think there would be a lot fewer problems in the world if everyone kept in mind how special God thinks they are—because then people wouldn't waste so much time and energy trying to prove how special *they think* they are.

JOE: Okay, let me put it this way. I have a very special problem and I could really use your help.

MANAGER: That would be the "no reservations" problem.

JOE: Right.

MANAGER: And you want me to help you.

JOE: Right.

MANAGER: Mr. Davidson, my motel is fully booked. I've been turning people away all night. Why should I help you?

JOE: Because God wants you to.

(The Manager looks at Joe in surprise, then smiles broadly.)

MANAGER: There we go! There's that living faith again!

JOE: Excuse me?

MANAGER: Most of the people I've turned away tonight have left here yelling and screaming at me, calling me all kinds of names. Others have just shrugged and disappeared back into the night. But not you. You came in here on faith and you're standing on that faith now. And I admire that. I really do. It moves me.

JOE: Thank goodness.

MANAGER: But it doesn't change the fact that I don't have any rooms.

JOE: Listen, Mr.—

MANAGER: Holiday.

JOE: Mr. Holiday, if you are the man of faith you profess to be, shouldn't you be supporting my faith?

MANAGER: Sure.

JOE: Okay then. You encourage me to go on faith, but when I do, you still don't help me.

MANAGER: I didn't say I wasn't going to help you. I said I didn't have any rooms.

JOE: I don't understand.

MANAGER: It's like any matter of faith, Mr. Davidson. Do you swim?

JOE: Don't I need a room before I get pool privileges?

MANAGER: You know how it goes. You think you've done everything right, you even think God has singled you out as especially dear, and you take that great leap of faith—and it turns into a belly flop. What do you do?

JOE: Get out of the pool before you drown.

MANAGER: And leap right back in again. Because you'll never get into the swim of things, standing on the side of the pool and shivering and concentrating on the belly flop. You've got to throw yourself back into the water and know that God wants you to be a swimmer.

JOE: God'd better be willing to teach me how to swim because at this point, it's all I can do to keep my head above water.

MANAGER: He'll teach you, Mr. Davidson, and you'll be winning blue ribbons before you know it.

JOE: I'm not in this for glory. I'm in it for love.

MANAGER: Love! Right! What kind of man leaves his pregnant wife in the parking lot? Go get her comfortable.

(The Manager tosses Joe a key. Joe catches it, surprised.)

JOE: But you said you didn't have any rooms.

MANAGER: I don't. But I have a pool house. Perfect place for a beginning swimmer.

JOE: Thank you, Mr. Holiday. God bless you.

MANAGER: God bless you, too, Mr. Davidson.

JOE: He already has. Yet the blessings keep coming and coming. . . . We'll always be grateful, Mr. Holiday.

MANAGER: You just take care of the wife and the kid and let me know how things turn out.

JOE: Believe me, Mr. Holiday, you'll hear all about it.

(Joe hurries out.)

Now a Shepherd, No Longer a Sheep

(From Sheryl J. Anderson, *The Twelve Plays of Christmas: Original Christian Dramas,* ©1999 by Judson Press. Reproduced by permission of Judson Press.)

The church fellowship hall. JUNE, CHARLIE, and JO stand together, looking over scripts, chatting excitedly. ANDY enters slowly, somewhat dazed.

CHARLIE: Hey, Andy. Over here!

(Andy walks slowly toward them.)

JO: Did you talk to the Pastor, Andy? Did you find out who you're going to be in the Christmas pageant?

ANDY: Oh, yeah.

JUNE: You don't sound very happy, Andy. Did you get a little part?

ANDY: Oh, no.

CHARLIE: I'm the cow this year. I get to talk about how all the animals bow down to the baby Jesus.

ANDY: That's great, Charlie.

JUNE: Jo and I are the two doves in the rafters of the stable. That means we get a song.

ANDY: Congratulations, June.

JO: So, Andy, what are you going to be this year? You've been one of the sheep for the last couple of years. I bet Pastor made you the number-one sheep this Christmas.

ANDY: In a way.

JUNE: The number-one sheep has lots of great lines and a song. That's fabulous, Andy.

ANDY: Actually, I'm not the number-one sheep.

JO: Well, the number-two sheep has good lines, too.

ANDY: I'm the shepherd.

(The others look at him in amazement.)

CHARLIE: Wow.

JUNE: Gosh, Andy. The shepherd!

Jo: That's a big move up.

Andy: I know.

Jo: Lots of lines and two songs and standing right next to baby Jesus for most of the pageant—wow.

Charlie: Are you ready for this, Andy?

Andy: I don't know, Charlie.

June: Of course he's ready. Pastor wouldn't give him the part if he wasn't ready.

Andy: That's what worries me. Maybe Pastor thinks I'm ready and I'm really not.

Jo: There's three weeks of rehearsal. You'll be okay.

Andy: But this is a big part. This is stepping out of the flock and talking by myself, singing by myself, telling really important parts of the story. What if I mess up?

June: What's to mess up? We've all been in the pageant since nursery school. We know the story pretty well.

Andy: But I've never had this much responsibility. I've never had to carry part of the story alone.

Charlie: You won't be alone. We'll all be on stage with you. If you forget what to say, we'll whisper to you.

Andy: Yeah, well, if people are going to have to whisper to me, I don't deserve to be the shepherd.

Charlie: We can all be shepherds. When the time is right. This is the time for you.

Andy: I don't know. I think I like being one of the sheep.

June: But you've been one of the sheep for a couple of years now. It's time to grow, to mature, to step out and stand up. You can't be lost in the flock forever.

Charlie: The other thing you're forgetting is Pastor asked you to be the shepherd. Pastor wouldn't ask you to do something he didn't think you could do. I mean, it would look bad for him and for you if something went wrong—

Andy: Oh, great.

Charlie: —which won't happen. Pastor believes in you, Andy. You should believe in yourself.

Andy: When Pastor asked me, I got really excited. I thought, this is what I've been waiting for. A chance to show what I can do. A chance to shine. And then I started thinking of all the things that could go wrong, of all the mistakes that I could make, and I thought: No, I'd better not. I'll just make a mess of things. I'll embarrass myself, I'll embarrass Pastor, and next year, they won't even let me be a sheep.

JUNE: On the other hand, you could remember that Pastor has faith in you and we have faith in you and you could do a great job and next year, you could be Joseph.

ANDY: Wow.

JUNE: Have faith. And grow in faith. And you can do anything.

ANDY: You guys really think I can do this?

JUNE: Absolutely.

JO: No question.

CHARLIE: You're the man.

ANDY: Okay, then. I'll do it. I'll have faith and I'll step into the spotlight and I'll be the best shepherd this pageant has ever seen.

(Jo and Charlie pat him on the back approvingly.)

JUNE: Oh, I don't know about that.

ANDY, JO, AND CHARLIE: What?

ANDY: You just got finished saying that I could do this.

JUNE: And you can. You can be a great shepherd. But I hear that the best shepherd *ever* was my dad when he was in high school.

JO: No way. It was my Uncle Phil when he was in college.

CHARLIE: Oh, come on, you guys. Haven't you heard about the year Mrs. Hart filled in because her husband got sick at the last minute?

JO: Mrs. Hart, the organist?

CHARLIE: I heard she stopped the show.

JUNE: In a good way?

ANDY: Okay, okay, so there have been many great shepherds. I will take my place among them.

JO: That's the spirit, Andy.

JUNE: Or maybe that's the Spirit at work in Andy.

ANDY: The Spirit better be ready to be at work in me. I'm going to need help learning all these lines.

(They all compare scripts.)

A Traditional Pageant

(From Sheryl J. Anderson, *The Twelve Plays of Christmas: Original Christian Dramas,* ©1999 by Judson Press. Reproduced by permission of Judson Press.)

Some years, classic is the way to go.

You may want to have the various performers enter down the aisles of your church and take their places in the playing area one at a time, building a tableau as you go. Or you can position everyone at the beginning, then reveal them with lights or by having them begin with their backs to the congregation, then turn around when it is time to speak.

THE PROPHET: The people who walk in darkness will see a great light; those who live in a dark land, the light will shine on them.

NARRATOR: In the days of Herod, king of Judea, there was a certain priest named Zacharias, and he had a wife from the daughters of Aaron, and her name was Elizabeth.

ZACHARIAS: And they were both righteous in the sight of God, walking blamelessly in all the commandments and requirements of the Lord. And they had no child, because Elizabeth was barren, and they were both advanced in years.

GABRIEL: Do not be afraid, Zacharias, for your petition has been heard, and your wife Elizabeth will bear you a son, and you will give him the name John. And you will have joy and gladness, and many will rejoice at his birth. For he will be great in the sight of the Lord, and he will drink no wine or liquor; and he will be filled with the Holy Spirit, while yet in his mother's womb.

And he will turn back many of the sons of Israel to the Lord their God. And it is he who will go as a forerunner before him in the spirit and power of Elijah,

PROPHET: To turn the hearts of the fathers back to the children,

GABRIEL: And the disobedient to the attitude of the righteous, so as to make ready a people prepared for the Lord.

ZACHARIAS: How shall I know this for certain? For I am an old man, and my wife is advanced in years.

GABRIEL: I am Gabriel, who stands in the presence of God; and I have been sent to speak to you, and to bring you this good news. And behold, you shall be silent and unable to speak until the day when these things take place, because you did not believe my words, which shall be fulfilled in their proper time.

NARRATOR: And when Zacharias came out of the temple, he was unable to speak; and the people realized he had seen a vision in the temple.

And Elizabeth his wife became pregnant.

ELIZABETH: This is the way the Lord has dealt with me in the days when he looked with favor upon me, to take away my disgrace among men.

NARRATOR: Now in the sixth month the angel Gabriel was sent from God to a city in Galilee, called Nazareth, to a virgin engaged to a man whose name was Joseph, of the descendants of David; and the virgin's name was Mary.

GABRIEL: Hail, favored one! The Lord is with you. Do not be afraid, Mary; for you have found favor with God. And behold, you will conceive in your womb, and bear a son, and you shall name him Jesus. He will be great, and will be called the Son of the Most High; and the Lord God will give him the throne of his father David; and he will reign over the house of Jacob forever; and his kingdom will have no end.

MARY: How can this be, since I am a virgin?

GABRIEL: The Holy Spirit will come upon you, and the power of the Most High will overshadow you; and for that reason the holy offspring shall be called the Son of God.

And behold, even your relative Elizabeth has also conceived a son in her old age; and she who was called barren is now in her sixth month. For nothing will be impossible with God.

MARY: Behold, the bondslave of the Lord; be it done to me according to your word.

NARRATOR: Mary went to the hill country, to a city of Judah, and entered the house of Zacharias and greeted Elizabeth.

MARY: And it came about that when Elizabeth heard Mary's greeting, the baby leaped in her womb; and Elizabeth was filled with the Holy Spirit.

ELIZABETH: Blessed among women are you, and blessed is the fruit of your womb! And how has it happened to me, that the mother of my Lord should come to me? For behold, when the sound of your greeting reached my ears, the baby leaped in my womb for joy. And blessed is she who believed there would be a fulfillment of what had been spoken to her by the Lord.

MARY: My soul exalts the Lord. And my spirit has rejoiced in God my Savior. For he has had regard for the humble state of his bondslave; for behold, from this time on all generations will call me blessed. For the Mighty One has done great things for me;

PROPHET: And his mercy is upon generation after generation towards those who fear him.

MARY: He has done mighty deeds with his arm; he has scattered those who were proud in the thoughts of their heart. He has brought down rulers from their thrones, and has exalted those who were humble.

PROPHET: He has filled the hungry with good things.

MARY: And sent away the rich empty-handed. He has given help to Israel his servant, in remembrance of his mercy, as he spoke to our fathers, to Abraham and his offspring forever.

NARRATOR: Now the time had come for Elizabeth to give birth, and she brought forth a son.

ELIZABETH: He shall be called John.

NARRATOR: And Zacharias' mouth was opened and his tongue loosed, and he began to speak in praise of God. And fear came on all those living around them. And all who heard them kept them in mind, saying, "What then will this child turn out to be?" For the hand of the Lord was certainly with him.

ZACHARIAS: You, child, will be called the prophet of the Most High; for you will go on—

PROPHET: Before the Lord to prepare his ways—

ZACHARIAS: To give to his people the knowledge of salvation by the forgiveness of their sins, because of the tender mercy of our God, with which the Sunrise from on high shall visit us.

PROPHET: To shine upon those who sit in darkness and the shadow of death.

ZACHARIAS: To guide our feet into the way of peace.

NARRATOR: When Mary had been betrothed to Joseph, before they came together she was found to be with child by the Holy Spirit. And Joseph, being a righteous man, and not wanting to disgrace her, desired to put her away secretly. But when he had considered this, behold, an angel of the Lord appeared to him in a dream.

GABRIEL: Joseph, son of David, do not be afraid to take Mary as your wife; for that which has been conceived in her is of the Holy Spirit. And she will bear a son; and you shall call his name Jesus, for it is he who will save his people from their sins.

NARRATOR: Now all this took place that what was spoken by the Lord through the prophet might be fulfilled, saying,

PROPHET: Behold, the virgin shall be with child, and shall bear a Son, and they shall call his name Immanuel.

NARRATOR: Which means, "God with us."

Now it came about in those days that a decree went out from Caesar Augustus, that a census be taken of all the inhabited earth.

JOSEPH: And Joseph went up from Galilee, from the city of Nazareth, to the city of David, which is called Bethlehem, because he was of the house and family of David, in order to register, along with Mary, who was engaged to him, and was with child.

NARRATOR: And it came about that while they were there, the days were completed for her to give birth. And she gave birth to her first-born son; and she wrapped him in cloths, and laid him in a manger, because there was no room for them in the inn.

FIRST SHEPHERD: And in the same region there were some shepherds staying out in the fields, and keeping watch over their flock by night. And an angel of the Lord suddenly stood before them, and the glory of the Lord shone around them; and they were terribly frightened.

ANGEL: Do not be afraid; for behold, I bring you good news of a great joy which shall be for all the people; for today in the city of David there has been born for you a Savior, who is Christ the Lord. And this will be a sign for you: you will find a baby wrapped in cloths, and lying in a manger.

SECOND SHEPHERD: And suddenly there appeared with the angel a multitude of the heavenly host praising God.

MULTITUDE: Glory to God in the highest, and on earth peace among men with whom he is pleased.

FIRST SHEPHERD: And it came about when the angels had gone away from them into heaven, that the shepherds began saying to one another,

SECOND SHEPHERD: Let us go straight to Bethlehem then, and see this thing that has happened which the Lord has made known to us.

NARRATOR: And they came in haste and found their way to Mary and Joseph, and the baby as he lay in the manger. And when they had seen this, they made known the statement which had been told them about this child. And all who heard it wondered at the things which were told them by the shepherds.

MARY: But Mary treasured up all these things, pondering them in her heart.

FIRST SHEPHERD: And the shepherds went back, glorifying and praising God for all that they had heard and seen, just as had been told them.

NARRATOR: And behold, there was a man in Jerusalem whose name was Simeon; and this man was righteous and devout, looking for the consolation of Israel; and the Holy Spirit was upon him.

SIMEON: And it had been revealed to him by the Holy Spirit that he would not see death before he had seen the Lord's Christ.

NARRATOR: And he came in the Spirit into the temple; and when the parents brought in the child Jesus, to carry out for him the custom of the Law, then he took him into his arms, and blessed God.

SIMEON: Now Lord, thou dost let thy bond-servant depart in peace, according to thy word; for my eyes have seen thy salvation, which thou hast prepared in the presence of all peoples,

PROPHET: A light of revelation to the Gentiles,

SIMEON: And the glory of thy people Israel.

NARRATOR: And his father and mother were amazed at the things which were being said about him. And Simeon blessed them, and said to Mary his mother:

SIMEON: Behold, this child is appointed for the fall and rise of many in Israel, and for a sign to be opposed—and a sword will pierce even your own soul— to the end that thoughts from many hearts may be revealed.

NARRATOR: Now after Jesus was born in Bethlehem of Judea in the days of Herod the king, behold, magi from the east arrived in Jerusalem.

FIRST MAGI: Where is he who has been born king of the Jews? For we saw his star in the east, and have come to worship him.

SECOND MAGI: And when Herod the king heard it, he was troubled, and all Jerusalem with him.

THIRD MAGI: And gathering together all the chief priests and scribes of the people, he began to inquire of them where the Christ was to be born.

SCRIBE: In Bethlehem of Judea, for so it has been written by the prophet.

PROPHET: And you, Bethlehem, land of Judah, are by no means least among the leaders of Judah; for out of you shall come forth a Ruler, who will shepherd my people Israel.

HEROD: Go and make careful search for the child; and when you have found him, report to me, that I too may come and worship him.

FIRST MAGI: And having heard the king, they went their way; and lo, the star, which they had seen in the east, went on before them, until it came and stood over where the child was.

SECOND MAGI: And when they saw the star, they rejoiced exceedingly with great joy.

THIRD MAGI: And they came into the house and saw the child with Mary his mother; and they fell down and worshiped him; and opening their treasures they presented to him gifts of gold and frankincense and myrrh.

NARRATOR: And having been warned by God in a dream not to return to Herod, they departed for their own country by another way. Now when they had departed, behold, an angel of the Lord appeared to Joseph in a dream.

ANGEL: Arise and take the child and his mother, and flee to Egypt, and remain there until I tell you; for Herod is going to search for the child to destroy him.

JOSEPH: And he arose and took the child and his mother by night, and departed for Egypt; and was there until the death of Herod, that what was spoken by the Lord through the prophet might be fulfilled.

PROPHET: Out of Egypt did I call my Son.

HEROD: Then when Herod saw that he had been tricked by the magi, he became very enraged, and sent and slew all the male children who were in Bethlehem and in all its environs, from two years old and under, according to the time which he had ascertained from the magi. Then that which was spoken through Jeremiah the prophet was fulfilled.

PROPHET: A voice was heard in Ramah, weeping and great mourning, Rachel weeping for her children; and she refused to be comforted, because they were no more.

NARRATOR: But when Herod was dead, behold, an angel of the Lord appeared in a dream to Joseph in Egypt.

ANGEL: Arise and take the child and his mother, and go into the land of Israel; for those who sought the child's life are dead.

JOSEPH: And he arose and took the child and his mother, and came to the land of Israel. And being warned by God in a dream, he departed for the regions of Galilee, and came and resided in a city called Nazareth, that what was spoken through the prophets might be fulfilled.

PROPHET: He shall be called a Nazarene.

NARRATOR: And the child continued to grow and become strong, increasing in wisdom; and the grace of God was upon him.

ALL: This is the word of the Lord.

————————————

(NOTE: Scripture is taken from Isaiah 9:2 and the Gospels of Luke and Matthew.)

Epiphany

Epiphany Mosaic

Depending on the layout of your sanctuary, you may want to perform this in the choir loft and the area in front of it. Or you may just want to put choir risers in the front of the sanctuary. All players are contained in the company and step out of choir formation when it is their time to speak, then rejoin the choir when they are finished. Costumes are hidden under choir robes and props are hidden behind each player.

(The company, dressed in choir robes, files in and fills the choir risers. THE CHOIR DIRECTOR stands before them, raising her hands to get their attention. On her signal, they begin to sing the "Hallelujah Chorus" from Handel's Messiah.)

CHOIR: *(Singing)* Hallelujah! Hallelujah! Hallelujah, Hallelujah, Ha—

(A SOLOIST bursts forward from the back of the choir. The surprised choir stops singing.)

SOLOIST: *(Singing)* Jesus loves me, this I know. For the Bible tells me so. Little ones to him belong. They are weak, but he is strong.

(The Soloist turns back to the rest of the choir, prepared to lead them in the chorus: the choir members shake their heads, muttering amongst themselves. As the Soloist raises his hands, the Choir Director puts a hand on his arm.)

CHOIR DIRECTOR: What are you up to?

SOLOIST: I'm trying to help.

CHOIR DIRECTOR: We're in the middle of a performance here. We have a message to present.

SOLOIST: I know. And I'm here to help you get that message across. And to make sure that it's the right message.

CHOIR DIRECTOR: Of course it's the right message. *(Turning to the choir)* Did you hear that? He's not sure we have the right message.

(The choir mutters amongst themselves again, some pointing to the Soloist.)

SOLOIST: *(Patiently)* I only want to be sure.

CHOIR DIRECTOR: All right. We'll show you. Get a load of this.

(Four people step forward, hands folded primly.)

QUARTET: *(Singing)* Happy birthday to you, happy birthday to you, happy birthday, dear church. Happy birthday to you.

*(The choir applauds madly, the Quartet bows and scampers back to the choir,
and the Choir Director steps closer to the Soloist.)*

CHOIR DIRECTOR: Well, what do you think?

SOLOIST: Is that all?

CHOIR DIRECTOR: Excuse me?

SOLOIST: I said, is that all?

CHOIR DIRECTOR: Well . . . Well, I . . .

*(The Choir Director looks to the choir, but they all shrug and look back at her
blankly. The Choir Director turns back to the Soloist.)*

CHOIR DIRECTOR: Are you trying to say you want more?

SOLOIST: There's a lot more to be said, isn't there? And even more to be felt?

CHOIR DIRECTOR: Says who?

(The Soloist taps his heart.)

SOLOIST: Says right here.

CHOIR DIRECTOR: Oh. Well, we can probably . . . I mean, of course we have
something else . . . Wouldn't want anyone to leave hungry . . . I mean,
you've only seen the opening. That is, we'll think of something. Stay right
there.

*(The Choir Director scurries back to the choir, which forms a massive huddle
around her. The Soloist waits somewhat patiently. Suddenly, ACTOR A and ACTOR
B are pushed out of the choir and to the front of the playing area. Actor A is
obviously displeased, but Actor B follows docilely along. They take positions side by
side. Actor A begins to speak, but is interrupted when two choir members dash
forward, pull the robes off Actors A and B, then dash back into the choir.)*

ACTOR A: *(To the choir)* Now just a minute!

SOLOIST: Feeling a little naked?

*(Actor A looks at the Soloist in defiance. Actor B looks down to make sure that
she does, in fact, still have clothes on.)*

ACTOR A: It's a bit of a surprise.

SOLOIST: A happy one, I would think. You should be grateful for the opportunity to stand forth as an individual and share the message of your heart.

ACTOR B: If I had known they were going to take my robe away, I would have worn a clean blouse.

ACTOR A: I don't like being without my robe.

SOLOIST: Are you any different without it?

ACTOR A: I don't blend in.

SOLOIST: You mean you're not hidden.

CHOIR DIRECTOR: I thought you said you weren't going to stir up trouble.

SOLOIST: I'm not. Am I?

ACTOR A: *(After a moment)* No. Not yet.

CHOIR DIRECTOR: Well, just watch it, okay? Now, let's get this show on the road.

(Actor A and Actor B are staring at the Soloist, but they turn forward and, taking deep breaths, begin.)

ACTOR A: Epiphany. A noun. From the Greek *epiphanein* meaning "to show forth, to manifest." Defined as an appearance or manifestation of a god or other supernatural being.

ACTOR B: Do not be afraid; for behold, I bring you good news of great joy which shall be for all the people; for today in the city of David there has been born for you a Savior, who is Christ the Lord. And this will be a sign for you: you will find a babe wrapped in swaddling cloths and lying in a manger.

CHOIR: *(Singing)* Hark the herald angels sing, Glory to the newborn king. Peace on earth and mercy mild, God and sinners reconciled.

ACTOR A: Epiphany. In many Christian churches, a yearly festival held January 6, commemorating the revealing of Jesus as the Christ to the Gentiles in the persons of the Magi.

ACTOR B: Wise men from the East came to Jerusalem, saying, "Where is he who has been born king of the Jews? For we have seen his star in the East, and have come to worship him" . . . And when they saw the star, they rejoiced exceedingly with great joy; and going into the house they saw the child with Mary his mother, and they fell down and worshiped him.

CHOIR: *(Singing)* Oh, come let us adore him, Oh, come let us adore him, Oh, come let us adore him, Christ the Lord.

(ACTOR A begins to speak again, but the Soloist interrupts.)

SOLOIST: In your own words.

ACTOR A: *(Startled)* What?

SOLOIST: Say it simply. In your own words. *(Turning to Actor B)* You, too.

ACTOR B: Oh, no. I'm afraid that's not possible. *(To the Choir Director)* That wasn't part of the deal.

SOLOIST: You can do it. Just don't recite. Don't quote. Don't parrot the words of all who have gone before you. Put *your* feelings into *your* words.

CHOIR DIRECTOR: *(Suspiciously)* What are you up to now?

SOLOIST: *(Quietly, but powerfully)* I am talking to them.

(Startled, the Choir Director backs off.)

All I want to do is keep it simple. Come on. Tell me. What is Epiphany really? Forget the fancy definitions and the angelic choir in the background. What does it mean to you?

ACTOR A: To me?

ACTOR B: Better you than me.

SOLOIST: Yes, you.

ACTOR A: As your representative, basic human being.

SOLOIST: As an individual.

ACTOR A: Is this a trick question?

SOLOIST: No. It's plain and simple. From one heart to another.

ACTOR A: I see. Well . . . I believe that . . . Actually, it seems to me . . . You want the truth, I suppose.

SOLOIST: Always.

ACTOR A: I don't know.

(The Soloist nods and turns to Actor B.)

ACTOR B: No! No! Don't ask me! Please!

(The Soloist looks at her in silence. Actor B does her best to look back at the Soloist a moment, then drops her eyes and points to Actor A in desperation.)

Okay, I agree with him.

SOLOIST: Isn't Epiphany something special to either one of you?

ACTOR A: Why should it be? I've got the big ones down pat, that's all I need. I know everything about Christmas. Ask me about Easter. I'm an Easter expert.

ACTOR B: I'm rather fond of Pentecost myself.

ACTOR A: Epiphany, shmiffany. Who wants to know?

SOLOIST: You *need* to know.

ACTOR B: *(Stage whisper)* Maybe you should talk to someone else. You're starting to embarrass him and he doesn't like to be embarrassed.

ACTOR A: I am not embarrassed.

ACTOR B: Yes, you are. You always get upset when you have to admit that there's something you don't know or understand.

ACTOR A: You don't know either.

ACTOR B: No, but I'm willing to admit it.

ACTOR A: I admitted it.

ACTOR B: But you didn't like it.

ACTOR A: And you did?

ACTOR B: It didn't bother me. Much.

ACTOR A: It wouldn't bother you much to admit that you didn't know anything, because you don't know enough to be bothered by it.

SOLOIST: Maybe we should talk to someone else.

(A TV REPORTER steps out of the choir, holding a microphone.)

REPORTER: Let's talk to the person on the street, a person with basic tastes and a common outlook, a person who mirrors the world around.

(A PASSERBY emerges from the choir and walks by the Reporter.)

Excuse me, sir. May I speak with you for a moment?

PASSERBY: Who, me? Oh, wow, you're a reporter, aren't you? Is this going to be on television or radio? Are you local or national? Is this CNN? Where's the camera? Be sure to show my best side. Can I get a tape of this when we're done?

REPORTER: Sir, I have just one simple question for you.

PASSERBY: Okay, I'm ready. Is this for the big money?

SOLOIST: You could say that.

REPORTER: Sir, as the average person on the street, will you please tell me what you think of when I say the word *epiphany*?

PASSERBY: Gee, that sounds familiar. Epiphany . . . That's the new Honda, isn't it?

VOICE A: No, no, he's the new place-kicker for Chicago.

VOICE B: No, they're a rock group. I hear their new album is incredible.

PASSERBY: I remember now. It's a new restaurant. I understand that their broiled sea bass will melt in your mouth.

(The Reporter and the Passerby shrug to the Soloist and slip back into the choir.)

ACTOR A: *(To the Soloist)* Come on. I'm not that bad. I mean, I know the facts. I know about the Wise Men. I can sing all the verses of "We Three Kings."

ACTOR B: Can you really? I always get confused with the frankenstein verse.

ACTOR A: Frankincense.

ACTOR B: Oh. That could be part of my problem.

SOLOIST: But what does it all *mean*? That's just more reciting. What good are dictionary definitions and pretty quotes if you can't feel the emotion behind them? Words are just the icing on the cake, the ornaments on the tree. It's the heart that counts.

(The PROFESSOR steps forward from the choir, carrying a thick book and perhaps chewing on a pipe.)

PROFESSOR: I'm glad you brought that up. In the work of James Joyce, we find a further application of the word *epiphany* that brings us to a closer understanding of what our friend here is trying to explain.

SOLOIST: Don't get carried away, Professor. Keep it simple.

PROFESSOR: Yes, yes, of course. Now, Joyce used the term to mean, and I quote, "the sudden revelation of the essential nature of a thing, person, or situation. It is the moment in which 'the soul of the commonest object . . . seems to us radiant.'" Lovely thought. Just lovely.

ACTOR B: I don't get it.

PROFESSOR: Epiphany is that one moment when you look at something, something you didn't fully understand before, and suddenly, its essential nature is revealed! You understand it perfectly! And that perfect understanding fills you from top to bottom and the whole world seems filled with purpose and "the soul of the commonest object . . . seems to us radiant." The heart is full, the emotions surge, the world seems right and proper because we understand. A mystery has been revealed and we have discovered a purpose. What a gift!

(The Professor returns to the choir as a SHEPHERD walks forward. He starts to speak, then stops shyly and looks around at the Soloist, who nods encouragingly.)

SHEPHERD: I really didn't understand at first. I was sound asleep and all of a sudden, there was light and noise and the most beautiful music I had ever heard and angels, honest-to-goodness angels, and they told us to hurry to Bethlehem because something wonderful had happened. We practically ran. And the sheep ran with us. Even they seemed to know that something special was going on. On the way, I asked the older shepherds what it all meant, and they said the promise had been kept, that our Savior had come, but I still didn't really understand. But when we got to Bethlehem and we found that stable and I saw that baby, then I understood. I couldn't put it into words then, and I'm not sure I'm doing a very good job with it now, but all of a sudden, I felt way down deep inside that everything was going to be all right. Forever. That somehow this little tiny baby, lying all bundled up in his mother's arms, was very important to me. And to everyone I knew. I felt so sure and safe and . . . loved. I knew somehow that this baby was going to do something wonderful for me. For us all.

(The Shepherd sets a drum down on the edge of the playing area and moves over to stand with the Soloist. BALTHAZAR, one of the Magi, steps forward.)

BALTHAZAR: All my life I have been searching for something pure and true that would at last make me feel complete. I have never lacked for anything; I have had my studies to challenge me, my treasures to delight me—and yet, I have been unfulfilled. I am not the first unhappy man to set out on a quest for the missing part of his heart, but I believe I may be the first man to truly find it. Along with my two friends, of course. We have found an answer that extends beyond the passing moment into the reaches of eternity. We have been guided here by God, led here by the star as surely as if God's own hand had been at our backs. God has brought us to the new King, shown us the glory and the wonder of a new beginning, and to the Father and the Son, I shall swear all my allegiance. I will give all I have. I will dedicate my soul. Would that a loving heart could be wrapped and packaged like a bit of gold or frankincense or myrrh, for this is the gift I desire most to give.

(Balthazar sets down an ornate box, placing it beside the drum, and stands with the Shepherd and the Soloist. The Soloist gestures to Actor A and Actor B. Actor B shrugs.)

ACTOR B: I don't know what I could give.

ACTOR A: You don't have to give anything. Christmas is over.

SOLOIST: What about giving thanks?

ACTOR A: Thanksgiving's over, too, my friend. You're running a little behind schedule.

SOLOIST: Is that how you live your life? According to a schedule? A neat, precise calendar that dictates what you can and cannot do? If you live in relation to a clock, time may wind up to be your worst enemy.

ACTOR A: I'll worry about that later.

SOLOIST: And will you give thanks later—when you have the time? Will you give God something in return for all his wondrous gifts later—when you get around to it? Or don't you have time?

ACTOR A: I'm a *very* busy person.

SOLOIST: Too busy to thank the Lord who gave you the life that you're so busy living?

ACTOR A: I thanked God. I caught Thanksgiving right on schedule.

SOLOIST: One day a year?

ACTOR B: *(Proudly)* Fifty-two.

ACTOR A: What?

ACTOR B: I thank God fifty-two times a year. Every Sunday.

ACTOR A: You make it to church *every* Sunday?

ACTOR B: Sure. *(Thinking)* Well, almost. But when you throw in the special days like Good Friday and Ash Wednesday and that sort of stuff, I'm sure it averages out to fifty-two.

SOLOIST: You're no better than he is.

ACTOR B: *(Hurt)* Are you sure?

SOLOIST: Going through the motions every Sunday or every holiday that you happen to make it to church still isn't enough. You have to feel thankful and express it and live it. Every day of every week.

ACTOR A: *(Sarcastically)* For ever and ever, world without end?

SOLOIST: Amen! Because that's how much God loves you.

VOICE C: For God so loved the world that he gave his only begotten Son, that whoever believes in him should not perish, but have eternal life.

SOLOIST: And what have you done for God?

ACTOR A: This is starting to sound like a stewardship campaign.

ACTOR B: And I thought Christmas was commercial. Is that what this is about? More presents?

(A SHOPPER steps forward with an armful of packages.)

SHOPPER: Presents? Presents? Again with the presents? Good grief, it's enough to drive you crazy! You know what my favorite part of the Christmas season is? The end. So don't bother me with Epiphany. Twelve days of Christmas are more than I can take. I barely survived the day itself. I forgot to mail early, so I spent half of my shopping days in line at the Post Office, and I'm sure that my cards—the ones that got done—all arrived late. My nephew's grown six inches since I saw him last, so I'm going to have to return that sweater and get him something else; my own kids are already bored with the toys they swore they could not live without; we've been to a party virtually every night since the first of December straight through New Year's, and I'm about to drop. How can you expect me to deal with another holiday so soon? Forget it. I don't even want to *think* until Easter.

(The Shopper steps back into the choir.)

ACTOR B: Is that what you want from us? Is that how we're supposed to be?

SOLOIST: No. Be glad in your giving. Rejoice in the opportunity to share. Don't celebrate Madison Avenue. Celebrate Bethlehem. Celebrate giving. That's what Christmas and Epiphany should be. God gave us the gift of Christ on Christmas. On Epiphany, we began to try to return that honor by offering whatever tokens we might have, whether it was a song or a box of gold. We have been trying to match God's gift since that first Epiphany and though we never will match it, never can match it, the effort to do so is one way we can show God that we appreciate our many gifts and love him. That's why you should give and be glad in your giving.

(The Shepherd and Balthazar return to the choir.)

ACTOR B: I don't have anything God is interested in. The Lord gave it all to me in the first place.

Soloist: Precisely. And what God wants in return is not so much material donations or concrete contributions, but the fact that you are willing to give, eager to thank, ready to serve.

Actor B: How? I can't do anything special.

Actor A: That's for sure.

Soloist: Love the Lord your God with all your heart, and with all your soul, and with all your mind. It's that simple. And that challenging.

(A DISCIPLE steps forward.)

Disciple: It wasn't easy. But then, no one told us it was going to be. It certainly couldn't have been easy for Jesus to go along day after day, knowing what was eventually going to happen. Even when he started to hint about it, none of us wanted to believe him. We wanted him to stay with us forever. I guess we thought if we wanted it badly enough, it would happen. So we followed him and we loved him and we watched him die. A man stood next to me at Calvary, weeping as though his heart would break. I reached out to comfort him, and he told me that he had seen the beginning and now, he feared he was about to see the end. I told him I didn't understand and he explained that when he was a little boy, he had been a shepherd in the hills outside Bethlehem. He was one of the shepherds that followed the star to the stable. And now, he was watching the child he saw that night die. We knelt and prayed together, and I told him what Jesus had told us. That this wasn't the end. It was a beginning. It was another birthday. It was the beginning of a new life. For us all.

(The Disciple steps back. A ROMAN CHRISTIAN steps forward.)

Roman Christian: It isn't easy. But no one promised that it would be. We hide from the Romans, live underground, and survive as best we can. The Romans make sport of us, burning us, throwing us to the lions and gladiators, but with each martyrdom, our resolve grows. Our sorrow gives us strength to work, to fight, to struggle on. We are determined that our faith shall not die away, that the hope we hold so dear will not vanish from the face of the Earth because of the whim of a human leader who, deep in his heart, fears us. I have no fear in my heart. I have only faith and the knowledge that we will be redeemed. I keep that in my heart like the memory of a special gift or a favorite poem, and it gives me courage. Surely God's love is the greatest gift of all.

(The Roman steps back and a MODERN CHRISTIAN steps forward.)

MODERN CHRISTIAN: It's not easy. Sometimes it's really rough. I mean, I'm not about to be put in jail for my faith or anything, even though Christians are still arrested and persecuted in other parts of the world. But it's still not easy sometimes. Some of my friends make fun of me when I go to church. They don't get that it's important to me to go to church, to be an active member of my congregation, to feel that God is listening when I pray. The world is changing, sure, and the world has changed a lot since Jesus was born, but Jesus hasn't changed. God hasn't changed. And people haven't really changed when you look deep inside. Everyone is still imperfect, still needs protection, still needs forgiveness, still needs love. And where can you get that any better than from Jesus? And all the Lord asks is that we love him in return and that we try to live according to God's rules. Now that sounds like a good deal to me. Sure, it's going to take some work, but the end result is worth it. No doubt about that.

(The Modern Christian steps back.)

SOLOIST: *(To the choir)* God the Father has given you his Son, the finest Christmas present ever given. On Epiphany, as the Magi gave before you, now you give, too. What will you give the Lord?

VOICE D: I will raise my voice in song to praise the Lord, for he has given me this voice and I will use it to serve him.

VOICE E: I give the Lord my unending devotion.

VOICE F: The Lord has blessed me with good health, and I will tend the sick.

VOICE G: I give the Lord my undying faith.

VOICE H: The Lord has given me riches, and I will care for the needy.

VOICE I: I give the Lord my everlasting love.

CHOIR: I give the Lord my life.

SOLOIST: Amen.

(The Soloist turns to the congregation and starts to lead the choir in a bow, but the STAGE MANAGER rushes forward, armed with a clipboard.)

STAGE MANAGER: Wait a minute, wait a minute. Wait *just* a minute, buddy. We're producing a spectacle here. You can't end the show now. Where's the pageantry? Where's the pomp? Where are all the beautiful girls on the white spiral staircase, humming "It Came upon a Midnight Clear?" Where's the vigorous men's chorus singing "Go Tell It on the Mountain"? What would Cecil B. DeMille say? I mean, I realize that this stage is a little small for the parting of the Red Sea, but we could get a nice little manger scene going here. You know, a couple of lambs, maybe a cow. We could even try a camel, depending on how the budget's holding up.

(The Stage Manager looks at the Soloist, who shakes his head.)

No? Okay. How about a laser show depicting the Star of Bethlehem in its ascent . . . No? Okay, the girls do an interpretive dance about the travels of the Magi. . . . No? Okay. Get this. How about we lower the Cherub Choir in from the ceiling and they'll have these cute little wings and haloes . . . Okay, maybe—

SOLOIST: Maybe nothing more than we already have right here—human hearts dedicating themselves to the glory and praise of God and love for one another.

STAGE MANAGER: But with no production numbers, no fancy sets, no marching bands, who's going to know that's how you feel?

SOLOIST: You will. And God will. And it's what goes on between the two of you that matters. As for sharing with your neighbor, a gentle word and a good example will say far more than a chorus line and a twenty-one-gun salute. All it takes is the murmur of one heart to another. And you can hear that much more clearly in the stillness. Stillness so great that you can hear the heartbeat of a child sleeping beneath a magnificent star on a silent night.

(The Stage Manager returns to the choir as the Soloist turns to address them.)

That's what it boils down to. Beneath all the fancy words and the shiny wrappings and the glittery celebration, this is what it's all about.

ACTOR B: Hey. It *is* simple.

ACTOR A: I don't think I can do this.

SOLOIST: With God's help and your faith, all things are possible.

ACTOR B: Christ not only died for me, he was born for me. He lived for me. He came to save us all. One at a time.

ACTOR A: I owe him more than I can ever repay.

SOLOIST: Pay him back one step at a time.

ACTOR A: I will live by his word and walk in his way and though I may stumble, I know he'll always be there. Not just on Christmas and Easter, but on Epiphany and Pentecost and the Fourth of July and every day that I live and throughout eternity.

Soloist: It's all related—Christmas, Easter, Epiphany, every day. Because every day is the Lord's. And so are you. And what do you have to say about that?

Actor A: Thank you, Lord!

Actor B: Glory to God in the highest!

(The Soloist gestures to the Choir Director. Standing next to each other, together, they lead the choir.)

Choir: *(Singing, from "Angels We Have Heard on High")* Gloria in excelsis Deo, Gloria in excelsis Deo!

WITHDRAWN